Fuchsias

in Color

Brian and Valerie Proudley

HIPPOCRENE
BOOKS, INC.

HIPPOCRENE BOOKS, Inc.
171 Madison Avenue
New York, N.Y. 10016

Library of Congress Catalog Card Number 75-18625
ISBN 0-88254-362-8

Printed in Great Britain

CONTENTS

	Acknowledgements	4
	Introduction	5
1	Fuchsia – plant of fashion	8
2	How fuchsias are named – some questions answered	17
3	How to grow them	22
4	Growing fuchsias in the garden	32
5	Protected cultivation – the use of the greenhouse	37
6	Preparing for dormancy	47
7	Raising new stock	50
8	Pests and diseases	56
	The colour plates	65
	Descriptions	145
	Appendix: *Fuchsia* species arranged in their sections	193
	Pest control chart	196
	Principal fuchsia societies	198
	Select bibliography	200
	Glossary	200
	Index of plants described	201

ACKNOWLEDGEMENTS

For their kind assistance we would like to thank the following
people.

Mrs Margaret Slater not only checked the names of the plants
growing in our greenhouse but also helped to track down many of
the raisers' names and often the date of introduction too.

Mr J. O. Wright of Reading has made a study of the species.
We asked him to amend the list that appears on page 193 and also
to comment on the species that receive a brief mention in the
descriptions.

Mr E. Wills of Chichester, the well-known fuchsia grower
allowed us access to his nursery at any time to photograph the
plants growing in his greenhouses.

The Royal Horticultural Society, London grows a notable
collection of fuchsias in their Wisley Garden and several of the
pictures are of plants seen growing there.

INTRODUCTION

Anyone who knows us will also know that for the last fourteen years or so we have made our living from the growing and selling of heathers (Ericas). Why then a book on fuchsias? Not everyone appreciates that to most nurserymen the business side is only one facet of growing; very often the other is growing for pleasure. To give an example of this, we have a friend, an expert when it comes to the production of high quality rhododendrons. His hobby is to grow vegetables. It would be easy enough for him to delegate this work to the staff who could, if required, move in with their machinery and other labour-saving devices to produce enough food to supply a small community. Instead the friend prefers to use hand tools and by his own efforts raise garden produce, moreover in sufficient quantity to keep the family supplied the year round. Our own hobby, if you have not already guessed, is growing fuchsias, not for sale, exhibition or any thing like that but simply for pleasure.

This personal interest not only in fuchsias but in gardening in general goes back many years, possibly starting with the tales that Grandfather told of the plants that he used to grow as a young man. The son of a gardener himself, or florist as the ornamental gardeners were termed in those days, he really was just how the old gardeners are often portrayed. Straw hat in summer, bowler when wet and long green apron were always worn when working in his garden. Pieces of bass for tying up roses and other plants could be seen dangling from his copious apron pocket. This also held a razor-sharp pruning knife for secateurs were something not allowed on his plants.

Starting work at the age of twelve in the garden of a large estate in Wiltshire, it was his ambition to be trained in the gardening arts at the premises of the great Victorian nursery firm of James Veitch and Son. In fact, it was the aim of every young gardener who had his sights set on 'getting on' to seek employment with them or the parent company in Exeter, for the best jobs in the land went to those whom they recommended. His apprenticeship over he returned to private service as an orchidist, but not before discovering and retaining an interest in fuchsias.

His first task at Veitch's was connected with fuchsias and he never tired of telling what that was. Like many old people Grandfather had vivid recollections of life in the past and never forgot what gardening was like in former days. There were tales of how pineapples were fruited in special glass structures called 'pine pits' – also the way peas and new potatoes were produced for the 'big house' by Easter Sunday and if not someone's job was in jeopardy. One task was to mount guard over a new orchid flowering for the first time. When it was exhibited at a London show the plant received a day and night watch to see that no-one stole a flower that could be used for pollinating another.

Fuchsias? Memories of these went back to that first job at Veitch's which was spreading fresh cow manure in the hot sun to dry! After several turnings it was ready to use or bagged up for the future. At the time of potting the now rock hard material was broken into walnut sized pieces to be placed in the bottom of the pot for drainage. By the time the roots came into contact with it, the breaking down process would have started, releasing valuable feeding for the plant. Who knows? Maybe this was the secret of the giant specimens to be seen in former times. At least one American nursery gives old cow manure as a vital ingredient in the formulation of fuchsia compost. Leafmould (leaf mold) and sharp sand in equal parts are the other materials suggested for a compost to grow perfect plants.

Now to the book itself. History is the subject of the first chapter. What fuchsias are, where they have come from and how they get their names is the topic for chapter two. 'Telling us that a sailor brought back the first fuchsia does not interest anyone' – sentiments such as this are often heard when growers get together to discuss their plants. Not all agree and speaking personally, we derive much pleasure from knowing of the plants and their background. How to grow fuchsias in the garden or greenhouse comes in chapters three, four and five; some other uses are also dealt with here. The reader may wonder why we have not devoted a section to competitive exhibiting as have almost all other writers on the subject. Our reason for not doing so is that we believe that success comes with the experience gained in actually growing the plants. Grow them well and the prizes can follow.

Chapter six is about keeping plants from year to year. The section on overwintering half-hardy fuchsias is written more for gardeners in Britain and Europe than for those in places with a milder climate, likewise the references to hardy cultivars. In favoured parts of America, southern Africa, Australia and New Zealand fuchsias will grow and flower almost the whole year round. Hard pruning has to be done if the plants are to remain vigorous and of good shape; it is normally done at the end of the cool winter period. If frosts are unknown then cutting back should be undertaken at the time the plants are at their least active.

Raising new stock comes in chapter seven; almost all fuchsias are grown from small cuttings or slips taken when the wood is soft and green. Sowing seeds is another method and may result in something new, perhaps a different colour or form.

The rather lengthy list of pests and diseases which follows in the next chapter might imply that fuchsias are a lot of bother in this respect. Nothing could be further from the truth for they are relatively trouble-free. Red spider mite and white fly are always waiting for the unwary: that is why the emphasis is on prevention rather than cure. Do not miss the point that it is essential to vary the pesticide in use now and then to prevent an immune strain of insect or fungus from building up.

Colour section

We are very fortunate in that the publishers have allocated a substantial portion of the volume to the colour illustrations. For colour and form we could hardly have had a better subject. Keen photographers may be interested to learn that 35mm Koda-chrome II film (25 ASA) was selected for most of the original transparencies. The other film used was Kodak High Speed Ektachrome (160 ASA) for plates no 76, 81, 84, 161, 178. A Nikon F2 camera fitted with the f3.5 Micro-Nikkor lens (55 mm) was used throughout. The shallow depth of field at close range demands a small aperture, so for the posed shots (all those with a sky or blue background) the lens was stopped down to f22–f32. A small aperture means a longish exposure on a slow film especially in dull conditions. We found that the shutter speed varied from one tenth second up to two seconds according to the amount of light. Except for the indoor shots of the hanging baskets at the Fuchsia Society's Show in London, where electronic flash was required, the subjects were lit by natural daylight, back-lit to be more exact, with a mirror to reflect the sunlight up into the flower.

Descriptions
Selecting a list of fuchsias to describe from the hundreds available is no easy task. Here one must be careful to see that it does not simply become a list of personal favourites. Everyone has favourites and we are no exception but we agree with whoever it was that said he loved them all – but some better than others! To form the list we have taken the catalogues of the leading growers in each country where fuchsias are offered for sale. Where a plant's name has appeared in two, three or more of these it has gone into ours. To balance up the selection we have added some new sorts which we feel will become popular in the days ahead. No extinct cultivars have been included; all could be purchased at the time of writing.

It is a well known fact that a fuchsia's colour or even the way it grows will vary according to the cultivation and whether it is grown inside or out. Whenever possible we have gone back to the raiser's original description to see if ours tallies with that first given and for this purpose the check lists published by the American Fuchsia Society have proved invaluable.

1 FUCHSIA: PLANT OF FASHION

Fashion is not confined entirely to the way in which we dress, for garden plants are as much controlled by fashion as are clothes. As today we see a revival in Edwardian or even Victorian modes of dress, so too can a renewed interest be seen in plants that were all the rage in those former times. The main difference between the two types of fashion is the speed with which changes occur. In *haute couture* the hemlines go up and down with familiar regularity but in the garden, changes take place on a much slower scale. Not all plants that were formerly held in high esteem make a comeback, for once the stock is lost they are gone for ever.

The Asiatic *Ranunculus* was one of the most prized of the old florist's flowers early in the nineteenth century when almost one thousand different named sorts could be purchased. Fifty years later the numbers were down to a score, and today? Today these formerly prized greenhouse gems are represented by just a handful, sold mostly in mixture. The double flowered exhibition hollyhock is another of the former florist plants that is no longer with us. Increased by cuttings only, these were named plants, unlike those of today that are raised from seed and sold too as a mixture or a strain. What of the fuchsia? The fuchsias so beloved of the elegant Edwardians could be put into the category of those plants that were formerly very popular and have now made a comeback. Many will not agree that this is strictly correct for they have been grown over the years, but we are speaking in general terms. One has only to look at the old catalogues to see the immense popularity these plants enjoyed in the late nineteenth century up until World War I.

The present day popularity of the fuchsia is well known to all, but where did they come from, these diverse yet easily recognisable flowers in pastel pink, lavender and lilac, flamboyant reds, orange and white?

Unlike many of our better known garden plants the fuchsia does not have a very well documented early history. In gardening books all, however, agree that the honour of being the first to grow and sell fuchsias in Britain goes to the nursery firm of Lee and Kennedy. These grew the so called 'American Plants' at their nursery in Hammersmith, London and were the first to flower the yellow *Rhododendron luteum* outside its natural habitat. Who better then to be the first to grow another 'American Plant' – the fuchsia? How James Lee, one of the partners, got his first plant or plants is where the account becomes the subject of much controversy, for each account seems to differ slightly from the next. The most commonly told story is of how Lee heard of an unusual plant that was attracting considerable interest growing in a window in Hampstead. At this time this was a small village to the north of London, and knowing of the public desire for something

[9]

out of the ordinary he made his way there to visit the owner and judge the plant for himself. He learned that it had been given to the lady of the house by a relative, a seaman recently returned from South America. Some bargaining is said to have taken place before money changed hands and the plant was borne back to the nursery, there to receive the attentions of the propagator. If this sounds something like a fairy tale that is because it probably is!

Another version of how James Lee came by his plants is completely different. This has it that he obtained cuttings of *F. coccinea* from the Royal Gardens at Kew, albeit 'deviously'. We know that they had a single plant of this species in one of the greenhouses for it is recorded in *Botanical Magazine* of 1789 that a Captain Firth had brought back a plant from Brazil and presented it to them the previous year. This fact is also mentioned in Aiton's *Hortus Kewensis*. If devious had the same meaning then as it has today it would not be the only time that good plants have been acquired and stocks built up in a similar manner, although on the whole nurserymen are a pretty honest lot!

Yet another version links the two stories by stating that it was Captain Firth's wife who sold the plant to the nurseryman. We suppose that if he had brought back several plants it would provide a simple answer. But no more of these theories. To have built up a stock of some three hundred plants in the five years before they came on the market would not have been difficult. The cost of the specimen in the first story we do not know, although the offspring fetched 'not less than a guinea, up to ten guineas according to size'.

The generic name *Fuchsia* had been coined nearly one hundred years earlier by Père Charles (or Carolus in Latin) Plumier, a French Jesuit monk. He discovered the plant known today as *F. triphylla* growing in the mountains of Santo Domingo (Dominican Republic). Père Plumier was a Minim, a member of a mendicant order in which the brothers owned no personal property but relied on charity as well as working for their existence. Born in Marseilles in the year 1646, he was admitted to the order when he was sixteen. He laboured as a wood turner, writing a book on the subject based on his practical experience. The study of mathematics was another of his interests and he took up botany as a relief from his other work. It was his great love of plants of all kinds that was eventually to take him to the Americas no less than three times, an arduous journey in those days. In the capacity of Royal Botanist to Louis XIV of France, he was searching for plants of economic importance.

Descriptions des Plantes de l'Amerique, his first botanical work, appeared in 1695 after his first journey. More interesting to us is *Nova Plantarum Americanarum Genera* produced after his third voyage and published in Paris in 1703, for in it the name *Fuchsia* appears for the very first time.

Some fifty people connected with botany in some way are commemorated in this work by having their names formed into generic designations. The name *Fuchsia* was a compliment to Leonhart Fuchs, a German doctor of medicine who as well as being eminent in this field was also a capable botanist, for the two subjects were closely linked. Sad to say he was never to know that such an important and beautiful group of plants was named in his honour for he died in 1566 many years before the discovery of the plant that bears his name for all time.

The reason that Dr Fuchs was known to Père Plumier was the existence of Fuchs' own book *De Historia Stirpium.* Published at Basle in 1542, it contained some remarkably accurate wood-cuts of wild flowers, including a plate of the Common Spotted Orchis *Dactylorhiza fuchsii.* Its present specific epithet (the name that differentiates between species in the same genus) also commemorates the doctor.

Latin is the language used today by botanists to describe new species. Writers in former times not only used Latin for the text of the books but for their own names as well. Fuchs was no exception to the custom: although he did not translate his name altogether, he did change it to Fuchsius. How similar this is to the names, both Latin and common, of the plant under discussion.

Plumier's drawings and text describing his finds went to the great naturalist Linnaeus who included the genus *Fuchsia* in his monumental work *Species Plantarum.* Plumier called his plant *Fuchsia triphylla, flore coccineo,* there being nothing unusual in a name of that length at the time. Plant names were a short description – this one means simply three-leaved scarlet flowered fuchsia. In his book, Linnaeus, using his binominal method of presenting the name of a plant for the first time, omitted the last part of Plumier's name.

Was *Fuchsia triphylla* brought into cultivation when first discovered? There is no reason to suggest that it was not, but when no economic use was discovered it would probably have been discarded. In fact, so inaccurate were the drawings in Plumier's book, that many doubted for several years the existence of the species described. Although obviously a fuchsia of some kind, *F. triphylla* was not rediscovered until 1872 in the same island where Plumier was said to have found the first.

Nurseryman James Lee started selling his plants of *F. coccinea* in 1793. So successful were they that the nurserymen who had purchased the originals, seeing the public interest, eagerly acquired new species as they arrived from South America. This was the golden age of the plant collector. If certain plants were wanted, collectors were soon despatched to find them and before long hybrids between the species appeared. All of these very early hybrids have disappeared, but a seedling cultivar that was raised by a Mr Gulliver who was the gardener to the Reverend S. Marriot of Horsmonden could be obtained comparatively recently, and may be growing in a greenhouse somewhere still. Named 'Venus-Victrix' it was a landmark in its day as it was the first to bear almost white sepals and tube with a contrasting bright purple corolla. Although nothing much when judged by today's standards, it was well received when introduced by Cripps the nurserymen of nearby Tunbridge Wells. Of importance too is the role that this small flowered chance seedling has had in the production of new and better cultivars, for the white sepals and tube present in many of today's cultivars have most probably carried through the years since 'Venus-Victrix' first appeared.

The cultivation of the fuchsia was by no means confined to Britain, for in 1848 a notable book appeared in France entitled *Le Fuchsia: son Histoire et sa Culture*. Written by Felix Porcher, it included a list of some five hundred and twenty species, hybrids and cultivars. We know today that many of these were in fact duplicates. This is not surprising, for as plants from abroad received French names confusion reigned when the plants sent to Britain were sometimes sent back under a third name. The publication of such a work does however give an insight into the tremendous popularity and success gained in the few years since hybridisation first started.

The nursery firm of Lemoine from Nancy, France, were one of the best known continental raisers and growers. They produced in the years from 1850 to World War I some splendid cultivars many of which figure prominently in today's catalogues. We think of 'Princess Dollar', 'Brutus' and 'Molesworth' amongst others.

Of the British growers, the firm of Veitch deserves a mention, for they were instrumental in promoting many new plants, both species and hybrids. Their collector, William Lobb, travelled extensively in both North and South America, sending back seeds of several important subjects. He is known best of all for his introduction of the 'Wellingtonia' tree, *Sequoiadendron giganteum* into Britain, but an earlier find was a plant that Veitch's flowered for the first time in 1847 and called *Fuchsia spectabilis*. It was found by Lobb in 1844 on his first journey to South America where he also collected large quantities of 'Monkey Puzzle' *Araucaria araucana*, another plant so beloved of the Victorians.

Story's were a nursery firm based at Newton Abbot, Devon. They were the first to breed a fuchsia with double flowers and also the first to bring out those with a pure white corolla in both single and double forms. One of their best known introductions at that time was 'Queen Victoria'. One of several plants with the same name, it no doubt proved popular with the subjects of the then reigning monarch.

By now there were in existence both a plant with white sepals and tube and also one having a white corolla. The next logical step would seem to be a cross between these two to procure a completely white bloom but plant breeding is not that simple. An almost complete knowledge of the ancestry of each parent, as well as a knowledge of the workings of genetics is required, before the hybridist can predict the likely outcome of his labours. No such information appears to have been used and for the workers who attempted the early crosses the pure white bloom must have seemed as remote as the rose fancier's elusive pure blue rose. It seems to be human nature to strive after something which appears to be impossible. Not until comparatively recently has this aim become a reality. The next goal is a deep yellow large-flowered hybrid. Will it ever come about? If not it will not be for the want of trying!

During the last century the art of cultivating the fuchsia reached a very high level indeed, and fuchsias were grown on a scale that will probably never be seen again. Greenhouses were filled, others graced conservatories, many were grown as bedding. Few were the great houses of the time that could not boast of a notable collection. Many kept a gardener whose sole duty it was to care for the plants, training them into columns, standards, espaliers and pyramids. In suburban villas they were used for bedding out as well as indoors and many thousands were produced annually for the purpose. These were raised in the vineries that ringed London where fuchsias were treated as a 'catch crop' to be sold before the vine foliage got too dense in summer. The metropolis has now spread out to swallow up the land where many of these glasshouses stood, but many of the plants they housed are still with us. 'Ballet Girl', 'Display' and 'Mrs Rundle' are some of the tough, free-branching sorts that were grown for the market trade as it was termed.

The coming of World War I brought great changes to every way of life. Gardens were especially hard hit. With the shortage of staff to care for the flowers the poor fuchsia was ousted from the greenhouses to make way for something more mundane – the tomato. The decline in general popularity had begun. With the war over it is difficult to see why an immediate renewal in interest should not take place. The fact is, it did not.

How was it that our plant was so soon forgotten when a few short years before it had been all the rage? It has been suggested that a rebellion against anything Victorian was the cause. In the new modern world of the early twenties the fuchsia, the tiny red and purple flowered sorts in particular, certainly comes into this category. Even today few plants can conjure up a better picture of the Victorian era. The breaking up of the large estates brought about changes in gardening methods unthought of previously, but a more likely reason for the fuchsia's decline is that many fuchsias had become extinct after being turned out of their warm shelter. This was the dawning of the age of the home gardener (as distinct from the cottager). The home gardener with memories of the magnificent specimens formerly to be seen at exhibitions and flower shows could not for a moment believe that they would grow under less than ideal conditions. Thus to the general public our plant remained in the doldrums for several years. Admittedly, they could be seen in public parks where neat formal bedding schemes often featured fuchsias. Several of the hardy kinds had already become established garden plants prior to this time, growing in the shrubbery or on the rock garden. Who has not seen the magnificent flowering hedges of fuchsias in the West Country, Devon, Cornwall, Wales and Scotland or marvelled at the vigour and cascading wealth of flower of these naturalised plants? Squeezing the buds to make them 'pop' will often be among people's earliest childhood memories. The cottage garden became a home for many of the favourites, while specialists have since found old, scarce sorts still flourishing in their refuge.

To pinpoint a general revival in interest is not easy as it has been so gradual. By the early 1930's fuchsias were once again being planted. A few years earlier in 1928 the American Fuchsia Society was formed. It is inevitable that when sufficient people have a particular interest in one plant specialist societies will be started. The fuchsia is no exception, for there are today societies flourishing around the world with a total membership running into several thousands. Being a member of such a group is of great value to novice and expert alike. The former will receive all the assistance required in the various aspects of cultivation, whilst the more experienced gains from the up-to-date knowledge disseminated from other growers through the society. In America there are three such organisations: as well as the American Fuchsia Society there are the Californian Fuchsia Society and the smaller Oregon Fuchsia Society. Enthusiasts in Australia, New Zealand and Rhodesia are catered for with one or more societies in each country. Britain too has its own, started in 1938 and now known as the British Fuchsia Society, with members and affiliated groups all over the kingdom.

Some fifty different fuchsia cultivars collected in Britain by Professor S. B. Mitchell were distributed to growers in California, both commercial and amateur, soon after the founding of the American Fuchsia Society and they have played a part in the breeding programme of the raisers there. The magnificent progeny of those introductions made their debut in Britain at the flower shows in the early 1950's. The fact that such creations can, despite their delicate appearance, tolerate not only the perils of an English summer but in some cases the rigours of a winter too, never ceases to amaze. Do not assume, however, that all modern fuchsias can be attempted year-round in a cold climate; several are not hardy, others display their flowers better with protection. The heads and stems of standards will not survive except in the really favoured parts. Nevertheless, there is available today a range of types, colours and forms with a vigour that puts some of the older cultivars in the shade. The hybridists in America and Britain, as well as other countries, are still busy producing variations. Sports occur occasionally too, to swell the numbers of good things to be grown, each year seeing the introduction of several new sorts. There seems to be no end to the number and it is difficult to know or anticipate just what is likely to be seen in the years ahead. Because something is new it does not necessarily follow that it is better. That is why many of the old tried and trusted sorts are still planted, so as well as being the forebears of the modern plants they too still have a valuable place in the garden.

For the fuchsia the future looks promising for there are few flowering shrubs with the ability to give such a return for the relatively small amount of cultural effort needed. They produce a wealth of colour whether grown in pots in the greenhouse or out-doors in the border or rockery, as climbers against a wall, decorating a loggia, in hanging baskets, or as house plants. All flower profusely in sun or shade.

2 HOW FUCHSIAS ARE NAMED –
SOME QUESTIONS ANSWERED

What is the difference between a variety and a cultivar? What is a species? These are the sort of questions that newcomers to gardening frequently ask. Although the answers will probably not enable one to grow better fuchsias, knowing the origin of the name gives added interest.

A species is the lowest basic unit on which the classification of all biology is founded. Two fuchsias of the same species will reproduce themselves exactly when, after cross-pollination, the resultant seedlings appear. Several species having only slight differences are formed together into a genus. Groups of genera (plural of genus) with general similarities are arranged into Families or Natural Orders.

Fuchsia is a genus within the Natural Order Onagraceae which anyone interested in wild flowers will recognise as the willow-herb family. This numbers among its members the familiar garden plants *Godetia*, *Clarkia* and the evening primrose *Oenothera*, weeds such as that pretty, but troublesome invader of shady parts of the garden, Enchanter's nightshade *Circaea* and also the willow-herbs themselves, some of which are weeds, but many of which are attractive wild flowers. These are all related to the fuchsia – first cousins if you like.

Two species within the same genus are sometimes capable of producing a hybrid when cross-pollinated, natural hybrids often occurring in the wild; intermediate in character between their parents, many make good garden plants. Natural hybrids can receive a cultivar name, but only when brought into cultivation. Hybridists using two, three or even more species back-cross seedlings with a parent. Once a desired offspring has come about, this too can receive such a name, after being propagated. Another way in which a new cultivar can come about is when a plant sports or mutates, giving rise to a branch or shoot that differs materially from the original. Several extremely good fuchsias originated in this manner, including all the coloured foliage forms.

What is the difference between a cultivar (cv or cvs in the plural) and a variety? The word variety was once, and still is for that matter, used to describe a cultivated plant that is now correctly known as a cultivar. Confusion can come about when using variety for these garden plants as it is the word that botanists use for a naturally occurring geographical form of a species. In *Fuchsia* this happens with *F. magellanica* in particular as we shall see later. These plants are not distinct enough to warrant the rank of a separate specific name and they are capable of interbreeding freely with the type. The Latin designation for them is *varietas*, always abbreviated in the name to *var.*

In some large genera there are groups of species which resemble one another more closely than others in the same genus. These are formed into series or sections with each section having a 'type plant' which is regarded as the most typical of the group. The genus *Fuchsia* is so arranged with seven sections. One of these, Eufuchsia, with fifty-eight species, is by far the largest, the other extreme being Kierschlegeria with *F. lycioides* as the single representative.

Here are some typical fuchsia names:

1 *Fuchsia*　　　*magellanica*　　var. *molinae*　　Section Quelusia
　　Genus　　　　species　　　subspecies　　Section in genus

This is a wild plant but also in cultivation in an identical form.

2 *Fuchsia*　　x　*bacillaris*
　　Genus　　　　Hybrid

The x shows that this is a hybrid or cross between two species within the same genus. It may be a wild plant or may come about in cultivation.

3 *Fuchsia* 'Enfant Prodigue' ('Prodigy') LEMOINE 1887 French
　　Genus　　　Cultivar　　Synonym　Raiser　Date Country

The name between the single quotes is that of a 'man-made' plant which is in cultivation only and is never found in the wild. Nearly all the fuchsias we grow fall into this group. A synonym is another name for the same plant (the example quoted is a mistranslation)*.

---

* Enfant prodigue lit. prodigal child

THE FUCHSIA FLOWER

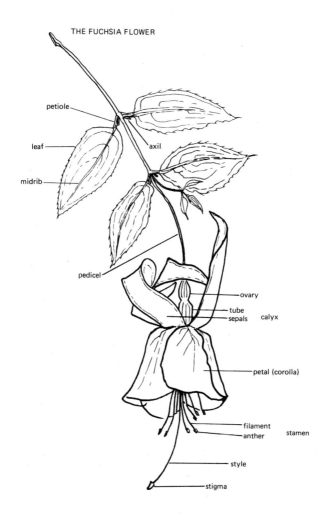

The compilation of the correct names of any genus as large as *Fuchsia* involves a great amount of research both in the field, in herbaria and often in the laboratory too. Anyone interested in our subject should be grateful to Dr Philip Munz for his work *A Revision of the Genus Fuchsia (Onagraceae)*, first published in 1943 by the California Academy of Sciences. Although basically a scientific work, it is of immense value to the keen fuchsia grower, for in it he not only revises the nomenclature of the genus as a whole, but also sets out the classification as we know it today, bringing order out of confusion in a masterly way.

With the introduction of species taking place over several years, it is not always easy to be certain whether a plant is really new to science or horticulture, or simply a re-introduction. Nurserymen have usually been the recipients of seeds sent back by collectors. In many cases they have not had the means of knowing whether or not they have been introduced previously. Several fuchsias have received synonyms in the past for this reason.

The naming of wild plants (species) is now in accordance with the 'International Code of Botanical Nomenclature'. The 'Rule of Priority', i.e. the use of the earliest given name for a plant, which has meant name changes for many fuchsias in the past, appears now to have more or less stabilised the names. The 'International Code of Nomenclature for Cultivated Plants', as its name suggests, governs all the names for plants we grow in our gardens. New cultivars of fuchsias are now subject to the code before acceptance. Briefly, the name should be new and not the same as one given previously, even though the original plant has been lost. The suffix 'improved' is frowned on, as is the generic name of another plant, e.g. *Fuchsia* 'Erica' is disallowed but *Fuchsia* 'Heather' is all right. The name can be in any language capable of being printed in Roman type, but not in Latin which is reserved for the names of wild plants. Many fuchsias have names which, because they were given prior to the introduction of the code, must still be used although today they would not comply.

The more important groups of garden plants have a specialist body to which application for the registration of a new name has to be addressed. In our case it is to the American Fuchsia

Society, who since 1967, have had the responsibility of checking names as a safeguard against duplication. They also vet new names to see that they comply with the code.

How many fuchsias have been named in the past? A difficult question to answer. One estimate puts the figure at around five thousand. This may sound an exaggerated sum but, if anything, we think it an underestimate. Fuchsias lend themselves to hybridisation readily and although not all introductions are winners for obvious reasons, good new cultivars are eagerly sought to join the ranks of established favourites.

Except for a few species cultivated in Britain in greenhouses only, most of the fuchsias we grow today are descended from hybrids resulting from early crosses between two or more species with *F. magellanica, fulgens, coccinea,* and later *triphylla* and others playing the role of seed or pollen parent. To trace the complete ancestry of the modern plant is impossible owing to the very considerable amount of breeding that has taken place, but in some there are features that give a clue to their forebears. The so called 'Triphylla Hybrids' with their distinctive flower shape give a good indication even if the parent were unknown. *F. magellanica* has imparted a great deal of hardiness to its offspring thus making fuchsias more popular than if they were only confined to the greenhouse. Only found in the New World, the genus *Fuchsia* forms part of the indigenous flora of Central and South America occurring down the Pacific seaboard from Mexico to Chile, as well as in other countries in the continent. The West Indies, New Zealand and Tahiti are other countries in which some species are found growing as wild plants. They are almost all found in mountainous areas, some at a great height growing in situations where the plants are subjected to a considerable amount of rain or cloud-borne mist. Those types that make their home in the dense rain forests of South America also grow in conditions of high humidity. The ability not only to survive under these conditions but to revel in them must be remembered in hot dry situations. The foliage needs to be kept crisp and turgid if the plants are not to suffer. Shade from the hot sun, syringing the foliage with clean water, and use a compost that does not dry out when the pots are left unattended for a while. Planted out in the soil the fuchsias are less likely to suffer once established, but even here a gentle spray in the cool of the evening is always appreciated.

Wild fuchsias range in size from low creeping plants up to fairly large shrubs or even small trees. Some are epiphytes, others vine-like climbers creeping up tall trees in a manner far removed from the popular notion of how a fuchsia should grow.

The flowers are produced from the leaf axils and are in the form of a tube-like calyx which is split at the open end into four sepals. It is interesting to note that all wild members of the Onagraceae have the parts of the flower in four, or a constant multiple of that number. The corolla of the fuchsia consists of four petals in most species, although in at least one, *F. apetala* they are absent. The dainty flowers are carried on a slender pedicel, or stalk; in the garden plants they are produced mainly in pairs but in the species they may be in clusters or a fairly large raceme.

Eight (rarely four) very noticeable stamens, each filament carrying its pollen-bearing anther, with the female parts – stigma, style and ovary – complete the flower. Unlike that of many plants, the reproductive mechanism is very prominent, adding considerably to the beauty and charm of the flower, in some cases the actual colour enhancing the shade of the more decorative part. The fertilised seeds are contained in the four part ovary at the base of the tube or calyx (tube and sepals). When the flower has dropped the ovary develops into a fleshy edible berry, rather insipid to the taste. In the wild these berries are avidly devoured by birds, by which means, after passing through, the seeds are distributed.

3 HOW TO GROW THEM

Several species of *Fuchsia* have been involved in the evolution or development of the plants we grow today. Not that this need concern us too much regarding the actual cultivation, but it does have a bearing on hardiness. Some are almost completely hardy, to be kept in the garden throughout the year as permanent subjects. Others need year-round greenhouse protection, or in those countries fortunate enough not to be subject to frosts, the use of a lath or shade house to protect from sun and wind. The bulk of our modern plants however, fall between the two extremes, with the ability to flourish in the open garden during the summer, although demanding warm winter quarters in cold countries including Britain. Even here, within this last group, are many that are hardier than is generally realised, which will usually come through an average winter with only the minimum of protection. Most are so quick in growth that it is perfectly feasible to purchase strong plants in late spring, enjoy a superb display all summer, then simply discard them when cold weather ends the flowering. They are cheap enough to buy so that many find it easier to do this each season thus avoiding the bother associated with storing the dormant plants. Of course, the results from older second and third year plants can be better, so we are not advocating renewing each season if space is available to store.

The selection of the fuchsias that are to be grown is made long before the plants are actually wanted. This is done by choosing either directly from a nurseryman's catalogue or from a list of favourites noted the previous summer. There is no better way of making a choice than to see the plants growing, rather than depending on a description in a price list. Try to visit one of the major flower shows. The leading specialists who exhibit at the larger shows are only too pleased to give helpful advice to intending purchasers and others. The Botanic Gardens usually keep an up-to-date collection, together with many of the older kinds and species too. Bearing in mind the varying uses for the plants, get the list off to the nurseryman as early in the season as possible. This will assist by helping him plan his likely needs of each particular sort. Those leaving their ordering to the last moment may be disappointed to find that certain kinds arc not available. You should state with the order the approximate time when you will be in a position to take the plants. Remember, they will have been grown in warm conditions and will need a similar temperature after arrival. Where heating is not installed in greenhouse or frame, it may be more prudent to delay delivery until the days (and nights) warm up a little, then just sufficient heat to keep out frost will be acceptable.

Collecting the young plants from a nursery is always best but if this is inconvenient or not possible, express delivery will ensure safe arrival. Unpack them carefully as soon as they are delivered, repotting into a pot of the size of the root ball, except where the compost differs materially from your own. In that case, it is better to remove most of it with much care and to treat the young plants as large rooted cuttings. The roots of plants growing in a soilless compost often show a marked reluctance to leave their little ball of peat and difficulty is sometimes experienced over the even distribution of water in the pot unless a similar compost is being used. Keep the atmosphere close by dampening down paths and staging for several days until plants have recovered from the move. Some people shade pots to assist in this, particularly when the young plants have been several days in transit; light syringing over the foliage early in the morning well before the sun has much heat will help at this time. The secret of success with fuchsias, especially during the growing on period, is to keep them moving without a check. This will mean a larger pot as soon as the first becomes filled with roots. One thing they dislike is to be over-potted (using too large a pot for each move which allows the surplus compost to become sour). A 3 in. (8 cm) pot should be exchanged for a 5 in. (13 cm) pot, then for a 7 in. (18 cm) pot (for a specimen). Many plants will go through the first season in the intermediate size, but older, larger plants are often put into 12 in. (30 cm) pots or tubs for the subsequent years. If potting-on is done at the right time the root-ball, with the exception of any drainage crocks in the base, can be left intact after each move.

In his fascinating book *Familiar Garden Flowers* published about 1890 the writer, the Reverend Shirley Hibberd passes on the advice given him, to grow fuchsias as if they were radishes. It may sound a little absurd to compare the two, but anyone who relishes them will know that the best radishes are produced in a warm mellow soil constantly moist but completely without stagnation. These conditions are exactly the same as the young fuchsia enjoys.

Fresh compost for the roots at each stage in the potting-on will result in production of stems and foliage at the expense of flowers. As fuchsias flower at the season when the days are long, the answer is to get through the initial growing period quickly during the early part of the year so that plants are in their final pots for the season and one can enjoy plentiful bloom as the days lengthen.

Composts

We mix our own composts, as do many growers, both amateur and professional. Over the years some quite weird concoctions have been advocated but although we make our own we keep to the formulae worked out by Messrs Lawrence and Newall of the John Innes Horticultural Institute (J. I. Composts). There are five composts – one for seedlings, four for potting. They vary from fine (J. I. seed) which we also use for rooting cuttings, to fairly coarse for potting (Nos 1, 2, 3 and 4). The potting composts differ only in the amount of fertilisers added, most growers regarding No. 2 as the best for fuchsias.

Some of the newer peat-based composts are excellent once the technique of using them has been mastered. The University of California (U. C.) have done considerable research in this field and have produced formulae to suit most plants, including fuchsias.

Ready-mixed composts

Potting composts can normally be obtained mixed ready for use. When bought in bags, the material should be neither too fresh nor too old before use. Many of these composts when first mixed give off gases harmful to tender roots owing to the fertilising element present. Others contain resin coated fertiliser which does not start working until the material has been moistened. Should the compost prove fresh it will be advisable to turn the bag out onto a hard floor surface (under cover) turning the pile at least twice at intervals of several days before using. In old compost the danger lies in the build up of salts in the material; chlorosis (yellowing of the foliage, damage or even death of tender roots) can often be traced to compost mixed many months before. Compost three months old should be safe, after that it is doubtful. We would be wary of compost mixed the previous season which is sometimes offered for sale.

Ready-mixed, the compost may be formulated in two completely different ways: loam based or soilless. Loam based means that the material contains a proportion of good loam, together with peat to provide humus for moisture retention and sand to keep the mixture 'open' or aerated allowing surplus water to drain quickly through. A balanced fertiliser is incorporated to maintain growth for several months. The most frequently pro-produced are those made up to the J. I. formulae which in our opinion are the best for all-round amateur use.

Making up compost at home

When suitable materials are obtainable, composts of high quality can be made up at home. A little more effort maybe, but often better than the purchased article and considerably cheaper, which is worth considering when perhaps there are a hundred large pots to fill! Loam, which for preference should be slightly greasy, is obtained by rotting down very thick turves cut from an old pasture. These are laid grass-side down in a stack, to be left for six months or a year before screening or shredding to remove stones and coarse material. Sterilising by heat can be done at this time, or alternatively with chemicals well in advance of the time of use. Not all growers sterilise compost for the growing of fuchsias, but as it is standard nursery practice we prefer to do it, for not only soil borne diseases are killed but weed seeds as well. The rough material left after screening can be put to one side for use as drainage (we call this roughage) in the bottom of the larger pots.

Peat and leafmould

The next ingredient is peat: granulated sphagnum moss peat is best. It usually comes in large bales which do not require sterilis-ing and is virtually weed free. Dry peat should be well soaked and allowed to drain before it is used; the easiest way to tackle this is to turn out the bale onto a level concrete area, make a well in the centre of the pile and fill with water. Sprinkle dry peat into this until all the water is absorbed. Turn the whole lot over, repeating the process until all is saturated. Leave the mixture to 'bulk' or swell for a few days, allowing it to drain completely before use. Leafmould can be used as a substitute or an alternative to peat. It should be treated to neutralise harmful organisms. The most satisfactory material to use is that obtained by gathering the fallen leaves of oak or beech and stacking them neatly for a year or more until they are of a light crumbly texture. Bracken foliage in a partly rotted state is excellent for fuchsias when it can be found in sufficient quantity. Both these materials will require screening before use; the coarse waste should be retained for use in the base of large size pots.

Other ingredients and mixing

Sand comes in many forms from ground rock to volcanic scoria. The origin is not important as long as it is clean, coarse, free from lime or other minerals. Soft pit sand with dust-like particles as used in the building trade is unsuitable, but their sharp sand is often perfectly usable. Most garden centres stock good quality horticultural sand. To facilitate mixing, use sand in as dry a state as possible. The feeding element is added by incorporating a mixture of fertilisers (except for the seed mix). For J. I. compost there is a ready-made formulation known as J. I. base. It can be purchased in Britain or made up using separate materials (see below).

Mixing compost

Assemble all the materials and measure the total to determine the quantity of fertiliser required. A standard measuring box can be made either from suitable pieces of timber or from an existing box converted to a rectangle with the dimensions 12 in. × 12 in. × 15 in. (30 cm × 30 cm × 40 cm). This will hold about 36 litres or one bushel (British) – the American bushel is slightly smaller. The weighed quantity of fertiliser can now be sprinkled on the top of the pile which is then mixed by turning completely at least three times. To ensure the even distribution of the fertiliser this can be mixed with the sand before it is added to the pile of loam and peat.

Composts for fuchsias

J. I. Seed For raising seedlings, rooting cuttings and first potting.
  By bulk:
  2 parts loam (passed through a fine sieve)

1 part peat (moist, medium or fine grade)
1 part sand (dry)
To each measure add 56 g (2 oz) superphosphate of lime.
Note: The small amount of superphosphate required per bushel, although not critical is not easy to measure. In practice one would probably mix a minimum of 5 bushels at one time thus bringing the weight up to a more reasonable amount to handle.

J. I. 2 For potting-on.
By bulk:
7 parts loam (passed through a medium sieve)
3 parts peat (moist, medium grade)
2 parts sand (dry, coarse)
To each bushel measure add 112 g (4 oz) J. I. Base or slow release general fertiliser. Some growers advocate a larger quantity of fertiliser than this. Our own experience suggests that using a lower initial amount but continuing liquid feeding as soon as the plants are established in their pots gives the best results.

John Innes base fertiliser
Where J. I. base is unobtainable the same mixture can be made from the following:
By bulk:
2 parts superphosphate of lime
2 parts hoof and horn (ground)
1 part sulphate of potash

Many report good results from the more recent slow release general fertilisers when used in place of J. I. base. These balanced materials have the added bonus of a wide spectrum of the trace elements which are so vital for plant growth. In loam-based composts made to the J. I. formulae these should already be present provided that the loam is of good quality.

Fuchsias like an acid compost
It is to be preferred if the compost has a slightly acid reaction when used for growing fuchsias. For this reason the chalk which is a vital part of the standard type of J. I. composts can be omitted when making up whether the loam contains lime or not. Should the loam prove to be slightly alkaline (containing free lime) it can

[28]

still be used for compost making if corrected. To render loam acid, flowers of sulphur should be incorporated in the mix. The rate at which this is used will depend on the pH of the loam. Try 50 g (about 1½ oz) per bushel measure: if the compost is still not acid the value of the loam for growing fuchsias is in doubt. An alternative method for correcting a compost and thus releasing essential plant foods is to water the plants after each repotting with an iron chelate such as 'Sequestrene'®. Used at the manufacturer's suggested strength it will also counter the effect of hard tap water used in watering. When liquid feed is given, this too will neutralise the lime which comes in via the tap, as it is slightly acid.

After mixing
After mixing, keep the prepared compost under cover, turning once or twice before using to aerate the material and disperse any toxic gases present. Do not use for two weeks after mixing or keep for longer than three to four months. The compost when used should be sufficiently moist to retain its shape after squeezing in the hand, yet it should break down easily when pressed with the thumb.

Soilless compost
Owing to the difficulty experienced around the globe in obtaining regular supplies of good quality loam and the variable nature of the material, several composts have been developed using peat and sand with added nutrients. Much of the pioneer work in this field was done at the University of California; their composts are known as the U. C. composts. Since the publication of the results of their experiments, many proprietary mixes have come into the market based broadly on their ideas. The main differences between these newer formulations and the traditional types which, incidentally, they have replaced in the majority of commercial establishments, are as follows:
1. Weight Generally speaking they are considerably lighter. This is fine when large pots have to be moved but they easily fall over when the plants grow large!

[29]

2. *Nutrition* They are lower in initial nutrient content which means that feeding must be started earlier.

3. *Watering* The aim when watering must be to avoid over or under-watering. In a peat-based compost this is far more critical than when a loam-based one is used. Allowing the medium to become too dry will result in the peat shrinking from the sides of the pot so that a complete immersion is needed to re-wet the compost. On the other hand if the compost is allowed to become too wet, as sometimes happens in dull weather, it may prove difficult to manage as it will take some time to get back to normal. A wet compost means that aeration is affected, a state of affairs in which the roots start to rot in extreme cases. Now that we have said all that let us hasten to add that these comments are by no means intended to dissuade anyone from trying these materials, but to point out some of the pitfalls to be avoided.

Soilless compost for fuchsias

Apart from the ready-mixed composts that are offered for sale it is possible to make up a good mixture at home using readily available materials.

Soilless compost for potting-on:
    By bulk:
    1 part peat (moist, fine grade)
    1 part sand (dry, good quality horticultural)
To each bushel measure add
    By weight:
    56 g (2 oz) J. I. base or slow release general fertiliser
    56 g (2 oz) ground chalk
    56 g (2 oz) dolomitic limestone (magnesian limestone) (crushed)
Note: The incorporation of lime in these forms is essential to prevent the build-up of acid salts.
For rooting cuttings use the above but without the fertiliser.

Choosing pots

The choice of pots or containers is a personal one. Some stand by the traditional clay but more use the newer plastic types. Clay pots have the advantage that they are porous, so that over-watering is less likely, although this itself leads to greater demands for attention during hot, dry weather. New clay pots should be soaked overnight and allowed to dry again before using. After firing at very high temperature during manufacture it will be found that they absorb a considerable amount of water when immersed. Watering in the normal way is insufficient to make the pots usable and any advantage of porosity is lost; the same can apply to pots that are painted either inside or out. Previously used pots, whether clay or plastic, should always be scrubbed clean and dried before use. Drainage can be provided by placing pieces of broken pot in the base of the selected container (polystyrene foam broken into small chunks is a good alternative). We use the rough material left after screening the loam but take out the stones.

Watering

When correctly made, J. I. 2 compost has a sharp 'open' texture that is free draining. Even so to be safe we advocate the use of additional drainage material, for fuchsias detest a soggy medium. The expert keeps the compost on the dry side when the plants are young, maintaining growth by frequent syringing of the foliage. Watering should be a good soak, then the plant should be allowed almost to dry out. Do not be tempted, as some are, to give a little, often, as this invariably leads to dry parts occurring in the pot. An occasional dunking of the pot, plant as well, will do much good as long as it is in full growth (but not flowering!) and drainage is adequately provided for. Leave the pot under the water until air bubbles cease to rise. The foliage which is rinsed at the same time is cleared of the odd insects that have escaped the sprayer. Most problems associated with watering a collection can be overcome by a. keeping to one compost. b. not mixing different types of pot.

Preparing young plants for the garden

There should be enough feeding present in J. I. 2 for those plants destined for summer bedding without anything additional being required. For outdoor work in Britain and Europe the shorter growing self-branching kinds are best as these require the minimum of staking. Before planting out they must be gradually hardened by placing them out of doors during daylight and returning them to shelter at night, in a short while the plants become acclimatised and can remain out at night. Wait until the danger from late frost is past before planting out in the position they are to occupy for the summer or permanently as the case may be. It sometimes happens that the shock of moving from the moist air of the greenhouse results in the loss of some of the foliage but this is replaced as new shoots appear from the leaf axils and should not affect the flowering.

4   GROWING FUCHSIAS IN THE GARDEN

When fuchsias are to be grown in the garden, the choice will be between planting out the hardy types permanently or treating them as summer bedding, in which case they are put in when frosts have ceased in the spring, to be removed after flowering has finished in the autumn. For permanent planting (this also applies to countries where frosts are not prevalent) the position in which they are sited is going to have a considerable bearing on success. Drying wind is to be avoided wherever possible, for under these conditions far too much moisture evaporates from the foliage to the detriment of the plant.

It is not easy to lay down hard and fast rules for siting the border, for fuchsias are individuals when it comes to their likes and dislikes. In general, the paler colours are better when planted out of the full glare of the sun while the deeper shades tolerate it better without spoiling. A bed that gains shelter from a fence or wall can be utilised in exposed places; a hedge too is useful to break the wind's force. In a windy spot without much shelter the shorter, more compact types can be selected. Try to position these where they can gain some shelter from taller subjects. The main consideration after shelter from drying wind is to see that they have a moist, yet free draining soil, well provided with humus. Although the hardy fuchsias will grow perfectly well in ordinary garden soil, it will soon become apparent when care has been taken in its preparation. Better foliage, flowers in greater abundance, better colour, a more vigorous plant more able to come through the cold season unharmed – these are the rewards for diligence in this aspect of cultivation.

Preparing the site

We must assume here that the reader has a basic knowledge of gardening, is capable of digging, removing all perennial weeds etc. without further instruction. Where vacant ground is to be used for the planting, a start can be made in the autumn. To give of its best the fuchsia needs a cool deep root-run, so, in light or heavy soils, plenty of humus forming material must be incorporated. This can be in the form of well rotted farmyard manure (FYM), peat, leafmould, compost (garden variety), spent hops, wool shoddy, (old rags make a good substitute!), anything in fact that will assist in the water retention when rotted down into humus. Even so, artificial means of watering may have to be resorted to in a prolonged dry spell.

Beds should be trenched, the sub-soil well broken with a fork before spreading the source of humus along the bottom and mixing in. Heavy wet ground will benefit from extra drainage which you can provide by mixing in sand or weathered ashes.

Do fuchsias need an acid or limy soil? The ideal pH, as the scale to determine the nature of the soil is called, is between pH5 (moderately acid) and pH7 (neutral) although in practice it will be found that they tolerate alkaline soils as long as plenty of organic material is present. If leafmould is used it is better to obtain it from other than an alkaline soil, for the pH of such material can be surprisingly high. The same applies to spent hops and old mushroom compost, both of which often contain lumps of chalk. Spent hops direct from the brewery, keeping that distinctive beery smell when delivered, are among the most useful of all materials. Use them for digging-in and mulching: there is no need to rot them down before use as they are completely harmless in their fresh state. With added fertiliser, hops make a good substitute for farm yard manure which is always in short supply.

Where the fuchsias are to follow spring bedding the area will not be available for autumn preparation in this way, consequently there will be less time to carry out the deep digging usually advocated. In this event it will be easier if the manure is spread on the surface of the cleared bed before digging in. The manure or other material being used should be at least partly rotted when using this method, for contact with fresh manure could be fatal to tender roots.

Type of plants to choose: hardy fuchsias

For out of doors, choose the more vigorous growing cultivars for preference, as they usually out-perform any with a weak constitution in the tough conditions they are likely to encounter. Generally speaking, the larger the plant when it goes in, the sooner a good display is furnished. For this purpose there is no reason why the plants should not be brought on under glass before planting out. They can be either grown from cuttings or purchased and, providing they are well hardened off, can be put out as soon as danger from frost has passed. In the event of a late spring frost occurring, sheets of newspaper will go a long way towards protecting new growth. Lay the paper over the whole plant, secure it with stones and remove it next morning. The same planting instructions apply to the hardy fuchsias that are to remain where they are planted; here it is even more important to see that they have a good start in life with a soil that has been adequately prepared.

Planting takes place when the ground is ready, with the soil in a satisfactory condition to receive them. Delay planting when it is cold or wet. Should the opposite apply, it is in order to water the ground the night before setting the plants out. When the intention is to allow the fuchsias to remain as permanent subjects they must be planted with the crown well below soil level as an insurance against frost damage. The depth will vary from 3 in. to 9 in. depending on the vigour of the cultivar. Fuchsias are what are generally termed 'gross feeders', a polite way of saying that they are greedy plants! They will respond very quickly to heavily manured or fertilised ground. The danger lies in the fact that under these conditions too much leafy growth can be produced at the expense of flowers. Worse than this is the possibility that stems will not ripen properly nor sufficient new roots form to carry the plant through the winter. At the same time they will require a light sprinkling of a slow release general fertiliser put on at planting and carefully raked in. Do not overdo this. The fertiliser will do its work over several weeks but should an added boost be felt necessary a foliar feed can be sprayed on the leaves once or twice during the growing season.

Mulching

A mulch of an organic material such as peat, leafmould (especially that made from rotted bracken) or garden compost, placed around the plants when the soil is moist will help conserve moisture, improving the soil texture too when it is dug in later. Granulated sphagnum moss peat is favoured by ourselves for this purpose as it is so easy to obtain and certainly gives good results. It has little feeding value in it so it should be used in conjunction with the slow release fertiliser mentioned above. Spread it on the soil only after it has been thoroughly moistened, for if it is used in a dry state, rain can only permeate with the greatest difficulty. Ensure that the plants never dry out by watering during dry weather. This does not apply very often in a normal British summer but in countries where drought conditions prevail it is more important. An overhead spray in the evening with a syringe or fine rose water can will be much appreciated by fuchsias after a hot day – a requirement that is inherited from their wild ancestors which receive an abundance of moisture in those countries where 'the rain it raineth every day and every night also'.

Decorative hedges

As a decorative hedge for summer display the fuchsia has few rivals, for there are not many shrubs that can boast of con-tinuous flowering from early summer until the frosts. This form of hedge is a feature of many coastal towns but there is no reason why, if care is taken with the siting of the plants, they should not thrive just as well inland. As it is intended that this is to be a permanent planting, extra work on the preparation of the soil is required. Dig out a trench along the line the hedge is to take,

[35]

placing the top spit to one side. Remove the second spit alto-gether and break the subsoil with a fork without turning it over. The trench is now almost filled with prepared garden compost or well rotted manure, trodden down and the top spit replaced. A sprinkling of steamed bonemeal is put on, raked in and the ground is ready for planting. Should the finished level of the trench be slightly below that of the surrounding soil then so much the better for this space can be filled in with a further mulch of sieved garden compost during the growing season. Place the plants along the row remembering to keep the crown (i.e. the point at which roots and stem are joined) several inches below soil level for winter protection. Spacing depends on the vigour of the cultivar chosen; 18 in. (45 cm) apart is the average. Pruning is dealt with later (see p. 47).

Other uses for hardy fuchsias

Hardy fuchsias are well suited for filling up spaces in the shrub border, where they add colour when it is most needed, and over a long period. Bold planting is the most effective treatment using at least three plants in a group. Each group should be of the same cultivar to give a really bright show. The coloured foliage of the hardy *F. magellanica* 'Variegata' shows up particularly well when planted with say *Caryopteris* or *Ceratostigma*. Interplanted with winter flowering heaths, some of the hardier cultivars give a good display when their jewel-like colours are set off to perfection against the green foil of the heaths' summer foliage. We have 'Alice Hoffman', 'Margaret' and 'Tom Thumb' planted in such a manner. They get pruned back to ground level very early each spring as the heathers are coming into flower. The new shoots of the fuchsias come to no harm under the protection of the dense cover of the heaths' evergreen foliage.

After the initial riot of colour is over on the rock garden in summer, there is often little to be seen until the late autumn flowering alpines are out. During this lull in the late summer the little fuchsias come into their own. These tiny growers, unlike many subjects planted for summer colour, have a perfect right to be included in a collection of alpines, for the name alpine does not signify that a plant comes from the Alps but from a high place. This many of the wild fuchsias do, for some have been seen growing at altitudes of over 10,000 ft (3,700 m). A personal favourite in this situation is the lovely little *F*. 'Pumila'. Plant them in groups in the full sun and they will not disappoint you.

5 PROTECTED CULTIVATION – USE OF THE GREENHOUSE

Owning a greenhouse, or in warm countries a shade or lath house, is a great asset in the successful cultivation of the fuchsia. Although by no means essential they give more control over the subject than is possible outside; for example where a greenhouse is used a start to the growing season can be made much earlier. Just how early will depend on whether heating is installed or not – a temperature of 13°C (55°F) should be the aim. An early start means that flowers are produced on a larger plant and over a longer period than can be expected from those grown solely in the open. Of almost equal importance to warmth for the growing plant is the way in which humidity can be controlled more easily. To sum up, the advantages of using a permanent structure for growing fuchsias is twofold. Firstly, for winter shelter, it provides a good start for the plants which will go into the garden later; secondly, it can house a collection of plants for the more serious grower on a more or less year-round basis. We say more or less because many do in fact stand their potted plants outside, and even more people bed them in the soil for a few weeks during the hottest part of the year when they prove a welcome addition to the garden display. To save time on watering the pots, especially those of the clay type, they can be plunged to their rim in the soil. When the watering is done it is an advantage to the fuchsias if an area around the pot gets watered too.

At the end of Chapter 3 it explained how young plants purchased from a nursery are potted-on into larger pots as soon as ready in order to keep them growing freely. Frequent overhead syringing keeps the foliage crisp whilst also discouraging attack from red spider mite. Overhead spraying may be stopped when the plants commence blooming.

Shading

To prevent the atmosphere in the house from becoming too dry some form of shading must be employed as the days get hotter. For a greenhouse, roller blinds that are attached to the ridge can be let down on sunny days or pulled up when dull. These are best but many simply resort to shading painted on the outside of the glass. Ventilation should be attended to each day in order to maintain a buoyant atmosphere with a good circulation of air. Temperatures must not be allowed to rise too high: the plants will fare better under cool conditions. The great fluctuations of temperature experienced in small glass structures are a big drawback making efficient shading even more important here.

Training

While a plant is still young a decision has to be taken on the ultimate form of the mature specimen, for fuchsias can be trained in all manner of ways, the outcome depending largely on the natural form of the cultivar chosen, as well as the skill of the grower. Strong upright growers make the best standards; lax trailing forms are a 'natural' for hanging baskets but are also effectively utilised for pyramids or bush forms.

In order to get the best from any given plant the growing tips have to be pinched out to shape the growth. This summer pruning as it is sometimes called can be done with the fingernails when the growth is tender, but if it is left a little too long a small pair of secateurs will do the job. Make sure that they are sharp!

Bush and standard

For a bush plant, the most popular form, it is usual to allow four sets of leaves to develop before pinching out the growing tip. When three sets have formed on the resulting laterals, pinch out the tips of the laterals. This will be sufficient for an average plant, but to produce a specimen of the type seen at flower shows impose a further stop after three more sets of leaves have grown. This will result in a superb well branched plant. Many cultivars will be found to branch naturally even without any pinching out, but these too will be better if stopped rather than left to their own devices.

[38]

A standard is really only a bush on a tall stem and has the advantage that flowers can be viewed easily even when the pot is stood on the ground. Planted out there is no fear that the blossoms will be damaged by soil splashing on them. To commence the training of a standard the single stem must be allowed to grow unstopped until the required height is reached. The young stems which are known as whips can be either purchased the previous season or grown from cuttings. In both cases they will need to be kept growing during the winter period to ensure a thick stem to carry the head of flowers the following season. A stout trunk will be produced by a strong growing cultivar, whereas one with a trailing habit will only be coaxed up the support with some difficulty. During the winter the young plants do not require a great amount of heat, just sufficient to keep the air above freezing. The more quickly a stem can be run up the better the chances are that it will be straight. Feeding with a liquid fertiliser containing more nitrogen than is normal for fuchsias will encourage suitable lush growth. This may be given at two week intervals but only when the young plant is growing freely. The nitrogenous feed may be alternated with the normal weekly feeding programme (see p. 43) until the whip is stopped for the first time. When a proprietary brand is used keep to the manufacturer's recommended strength without trying to hurry things along. Stems are usually allowed to reach 36 in.–40 in. high before removing the growing tip. Pinch out at least twice more each time the laterals make three or four sets of leaves. A better head will develop from a stem that produces leaves in threes rather than the usual pairs and these plants can often be selected when still in the young stage. Side growths that develop on the main stem below the head must be removed as they appear taking care to leave the foliage intact; this is not taken off until the training is complete with the flowers about to appear.

Standards are always staked securely throughout their life. Where several are being grown the individual canes can be tied to a cross wire to prevent accidental damage while growth is still very soft.

[39]

Basket, fan and climber

Hanging baskets, either circular or semicircular, are a fine way of growing fuchsias and the pendant growth of many of the best cultivars lends itself to this type of feature. Here, the cascading flowers can trail with no fear of becoming damaged as they could be if planted in the soil. A well-filled round basket planted with say three plants of the current season, or a good size specimen in a half basket will make a colourful display in the greenhouse, patio or porch. Keep to one cultivar in each container, for when mixed, the varying rate of growth of each plant can lead to a lop-sided effect. The growing season needs to be fairly long if the baskets are needed for display over the greater part of the summer. This makes the greenhouse essential in the early stages although it is not needed when well grown plants are purchased ready for filling the basket. For the really pendant cultivars the small plants are started in pots and allowed to produce four sets of leaves before stopping. Only two of the resulting shoots are retained. These are encouraged to grow without further stopping so that when put into the basket they reach the rim before breaking. Pinching-out is done as each shoot reaches the three leaf stage. Timing the flowers so that they open on a certain date can be done by remembering that it will take about six weeks from the time of the last stop. If flower buds are removed up to this time the final display will be the better for it.

Fuchsias in baskets require a great deal of water in a dry spell. Under these conditions every evening will not be too often to take the basket down. Half immerse it in water until saturated, allowing it to drain before replacing. While the basket is down go over the plants to check for insect pests, remove spent flowers and dead foliage.

A fan-trained fuchsia can, with skill, be induced to cover a wall or fence in a relatively short time if a strong grower is selected. Start the training with a young plant, allowing it to grow three sets of leaves before pinching out the tip. Using a light framework for support, tie in the resultant breaks carefully before stopping the growth again when a further three sets of leaves have developed. Always choose the strongest shoot that grows at each break, tying it in to form the rays of a fan. Remove unwanted growth altogether and keep the laterals that will bear the flowers pinched well back until the shape is well formed.

Another method of training some fuchsias is to treat them as climbers. They are not climbers in the true sense of the word so will need to be pinched back and tied in carefully until they cover the roof supports with their mass of pendulous flowers. Looking up into the blooms from below one gets a completely different impression of their shape and colouration, which makes this way of growing so worth while where the right conditions for winter protection are possible. A vigorous growing young plant is allowed to grow away with a single leader by removing side growths as they appear. Once the leader has grown to a reasonable height, two lateral shoots are left to develop and are tied in with it. (The height at which the climber is allowed to keep these side growths depends on the position in which it is planted: sometimes they will be left just above the ground level but more often from above the staging.) Pruning consists of spurring back all side growths to one or two buds in winter and pinching out the tips of new shoots twice to ensure plenty of flowering wood.

The pyramid shape is not for the beginner but with experience it will make a fine way of growing a specimen plant that will, with care, last for many seasons. Some pyramids we have seen are really a bush shape with a standard growing on the same root. Very briefly (for each has his own method of getting such a result) the training is as follows. An unstopped shoot is tied loosely to a strong stake and is allowed to run up to 12 in. (30 cm), then stopped. All the laterals are pinched out as soon as they have formed two sets of leaves with the exception of one of the topmost shoots, the strongest, which is tied-in to the stake to make a new leader. This in turn is stopped when the required height has been reached with all of its laterals pinched back as they each form two sets of leaves. An experienced grower will, by the time the flowering starts, have a mass of blooms from the laterals spaced nicely around the well-supported plant which tapers from the base to the tip. A 'cascade' or trailing cultivar is often used with spectacular results although it will require much work and will need two complete seasons with a dormant period in between before the effect is achieved.

The column shape is another way of growing fuchsias in which the expert pits his skill against the plant's natural reluctance to grow in a narrow column, for left to themselves most plants would grow into a loose bush, whilst others would trail about over the ground. A column will need a strong grower, a strong stake and a strong will, for this is another form that takes a minimum of two seasons' growth to obtain. There is more than one way of obtaining the desired form but the easiest is to tie an unstopped plant to the stake, pinching back the laterals to a single pair of leaves as they are formed. The secret is to be able to time the flowering so that all the flowers open at the same time. The only way to ensure this is to see that each lateral is stopped on the same occasion, allowing a minimum of six weeks to flowering time.

The training that is carried out in the first season sets the pattern for the whole of the life of the plant and once spoiled the shape is often difficult to rectify, although if a mistake occurs one can usually turn a plant back into a bush shape. Many taking up the growing of fuchsias for the first time are a little dubious about pinching out nice growing tips or removing flower buds from immature plants. What must be remembered about growing this group of plants in pots is that it is an unnatural life for them, and therefore they are subject to methods that are not used for plants growing in the soil.

Staking

Many of the half-hardy summer bedding fuchsias, as well as those used for greenhouse decoration, will be better if supported. All that is required is a light cane with a single loop of wool right round the plant. Try to keep any canes as unobtrusive as possible, otherwise the decorative effect of the plant will be spoiled.

Standards, whether indoors or out, will always need a stake, in this case extending the height of the stem including the head. The head, once developed, should also receive some additional support from stiff wires extending from the top of the stake down and outwards rather in the fashion of the ribs of an umbrella, although not as numerous. If the end of the wire is bent into a tight hook each main lateral can be lifted over it carefully before the opening flowers develop much weight. This considerably lessens the risk of shedding a branch. For those plants that are destined for hanging baskets, the light cane support is removed when the fuchsia has been planted in the basket, and the stems can then trail over in a natural manner.

A single cane is needed for pyramids, but be prepared to give additional support with wires to the lower or central parts of the plants if necessary. The taller the fuchsia is allowed to go the more support is likely to be needed.

When fuchsias are being trained in a fan shape, a light framework is employed when the young plant is still in a pot prior to planting out. Wires stretched between suitable nails fixed to the fence or wall can cover the area the mature shrub is likely to reach. These are fixed in position before the plant is set out. The temporary framework used with the pot grown plant is removed at planting time when the partly trained branches are tied in lightly with soft wool along the wire supports.

Some of the cultivars that are grown inside will be better for supporting. When starting off the supports should be of the lightest cane, getting more substantial as the plant matures. Insert the sharpened stake with great care to avoid damaging fleshy roots. Several materials are suitable for tying, e.g. wool or raffia. We use ready-made covered wire ties which are very quick in use, only needing a single twist to secure or remove. Be careful not to restrict the flow of the sap by tying too tightly, for tiny stems can swell considerably during the course of a full season.

Feeding

Pot grown fuchsias are among the few plants that really need feeding throughout their growing season. In addition to the solid fertiliser contained in the compost, a liquid feed will ensure a continuance of satisfactory growth with flowers of better colour and more substance. Where plants are growing in soilless composts, extra feeding is even more important owing to their initial lower nutrient content. Although solid material can be used to give that added boost, more control is made available by using liquid feeding which is immediately taken up by the plant. An application once a week will be in order when the plants are growing freely except where repotting has just been done. Use a preparation with a high potash content (K_2O) to ensure plentiful flowers carried on solid stems. As with all feeding of plants a little now and then is better than a heavy dose at infrequent intervals. Should the plant be unable to take up the proffered nutrient for some reason or other, the leaves take on a yellowish hue with distinct green veining. When this happens, discontinue application until foliage returns to normal. There are some cultivars in which a slight yellowing of the foliage is perfectly normal; the very beautiful 'Morning Light' is one of these. Another occasion when foliage turns the wrong colour, in this case purplish, is when plants are taken from a warm greenhouse into colder outdoor conditions. Except in extreme cases plants make a good recovery to flower normally during the season.

Other ways of growing fuchsias in the greenhouse

Nearly all fuchsias seen inside are either in pots or hanging in baskets, but they need not be confined to this way of growing. Planting directly in a border that has been well prepared is one of the easiest methods of cultivation and certainly the finest way of displaying them in a natural manner. Imagination plays a big part in the ultimate success of a fuchsia border, for the grouping of the colours so that they harmonise is most important. To commence, the plants are grown normally in pots until well established and are trained for bush shape and so on as required. Tall growers, perhaps with a standard or two are planted in the centre of the bed first to give height. Bush forms are kept near the front, together with trailers which should be at the edge near the path. It may be that the border is not very wide, in which case the taller growers will have to be alternated with the low or more compact forms. Where there is a wall to the rear a fan-trained specimen will provide a good backdrop.

Should any other plants be put in with the fuchsias? This is a personal decision. Ferns of many species, *Coleus*, *Impatiens*, etc. are all natural companions, although we feel that the enthusiast will want to grow as many fuchsias as he can from the wide range available including the fascinating species. A border planted with fuchsias in this way need not be regarded as a temporary home, for provided the soil is in good heart when they go in, the fuchsias

[44]

will last and thrive for many seasons. The occasional ailing specimen can be taken out to be replaced with something new that has caught the eye. Do not crowd the plants when first setting out, for they do not care for too much competition at the roots, nor do the flowers display as well when branches intertwine. Most fuchsias are not really hot house plants but the best flowers are seen in cooler conditions. This is a help in winter for they do not need much heat. Provided that the temperature does not drop below 5°C (40°F) they should come through unharmed. Some of the species are better off at slightly higher temperatures than these, making artificial heating a 'must'. Water sparingly during the cold months so that the plants become semi-dormant. When the warmer days start up in the spring, pruning can be done according to needs, a dressing of a complete fertiliser given and a mulch of fresh soil or well rotted manure spread over the bed.

There are far too many different kinds of fuchsias suited to greenhouse display to be able to recommend a selection. The descriptive list that follows the colour section deals with a wide range of the more popular of these. In the cold greenhouse (or shade house in a warm climate) fuchsias are best treated in the same way as the more tender sorts used outdoors, that is to say they must be allowed to become dormant after the main flowering is over and stored in a frost free situation until starting up again in the spring. (For more details see p. 49). Pot plants display better if grown on staging rather than on the floor. Not only is management easier at this height but the flowers are nearer eye level and can be viewed more easily. Do not crowd the pots on the staging, for the individual plants will grow better with less likelihood of pests being overlooked when they are spaced out. Give the pots a half turn every few days to get a nicely balanced plant, for otherwise they tend to grow towards the light on one side.

Try them in baskets
Hanging baskets can be purchased, made from galvanised wire, plastic or wood. Our own favourites are the teak baskets normally used for the culture of orchids, which display fuchsias in a most

natural manner. Except for some of the plastic types a lining of green moss is placed first to stop the compost from washing through. Where this is difficult to come by, green polythene has been used as a substitute.

No greenhouse? This need not deter anyone from growing fuchsias in pots for use on the patio or in window boxes. Treatment is basically the same as when they are grown in a cold greenhouse. Young plants are purchased in the spring, potted-on as required using a cold frame or even a window-sill for the early stages. When the summer is over they can be discarded or stored in a frost-free place until the following spring. Growth is restarted by bringing them out, watering, pruning and repotting (see p. 50).

House plants
Many of the large flowered modern cultivars of fuchsia that grace our greenhouse do not take kindly to cultivation in the home as a house plant. They invariably show their displeasure first of all by dropping all their flowers as soon as they are brought indoors, then soon afterwards shedding their foliage. Yet the Victorian housewives used the fuchsia with great success. What was their secret? – for in spite of flickering gas lights, the greatest killer of all house plants, many thousands are said to have been purchased for this purpose. It is the dry atmosphere present in today's homes that is their dislike, for the murky conditions present in the previous era suited the fuchsias more than the light, bright atmosphere we all enjoy today. The type of plants they used were of the smaller-flowered, almost hardy kinds that can still be purchased. Try 'Princess Dollar', 'Port Arthur' or 'Gloire de Marche'. If these are selected, placed on a gravel tray in light conditions but not too sunny, there is no reason why they cannot be used as flowering house plants. They must never be allowed to dry out when in active growth but as the days grow shorter less water may be given. Dormancy is finally brought about by withholding water almost altogether. Pots may be stood outside in sunny weather to ripen the wood before they are placed in a cupboard, shed or cellar until the spring. Repotting is not as important for house plant fuchsias as for those in the greenhouse,

for as long as some of the old compost is replaced with fresh each spring the plants should thrive, but they must be pruned back well each year. Like many other house plants, fuchsias enjoy being stood outside in a gentle shower, but do not wait for rain to cleanse the foliage. This should be done regularly with a piece of cotton wool soaked in water. Regular feeding is important to maintain active growth and a watch should be kept for pests of which greenfly is usually the most troublesome.

6   PREPARING FOR DORMANCY

In the autumn, after a frost has burned the foliage, it will be time to prepare the outdoor fuchsias for their dormant or resting period. Except in the very mildest climate some form of protection will be advisable even for the hardy cultivars. On the rockery or in the shrub border it is normally enough to draw some of the surrounding soil towards the centre of the plant so that the crown is well covered. A layer of dry peat 6 in. (15 cm) deep will prove a good insulation against most frosts; some flat stones can be laid on this leaving the crown clear. These stones will hold the material in place until the spring when they can be removed, while the peat which remains will act as a mulch. At the same time the stems are pruned back to living wood and the new shoots will grow away strongly even if the plant has been cut by frost almost to ground level.

Where established hedges are concerned a little more attention is needed. Here, as in the case of single plants, draw soil over the crowns; peat or weathered ash may be used instead. At the same time, weave dry bracken or straw in and around the lower stems to protect them from the worst of the weather. In really cold gardens plants may also require a sheet of polythene to be secured around the outside in a tent-like fashion. Plants trained against a wall are usually much safer from the effects of harsh weather than similar plants in the open, although even here it is good sense to provide some cover for the lower stems down to soil level. This insulation remains in position until the spring when the bracken or straw is removed carefully to avoid damaging the emerging shoots. In instances where plants have been found to have been killed back, delay the pruning until the extent of the damage is clearly seen. Where a hedge has come through the dormant time well, most of the framework of branches will be intact. The time to prune will be when new shoots are seen breaking into growth. Take off all weak, thin or badly placed stems of the previous season and reduce any dead branches back to living wood.

Summer bedders

A different treatment is accorded to those fuchsias that have been grown as summer bedding. These are unable to remain in their positions for other plants will occupy the space they vacate ready for the spring display. As with the hardy cultivars, wait until shorter days terminate growth for the season before lifting the plants which need a frost free place for the winter. This can be a greenhouse, cold-frame, shed or cellar – some enthusiasts have even been known to accommodate them in a spare bedroom! After lifting, place the plants in an airy spot to allow the soil surrounding the root ball to become partially dry. Before plunging in leaves, bracken, straw or peat the plants should be tidied up by reducing the size of the root ball, trimming off withered shoots or broken growths. Do not allow the roots to become totally dry at any time during the dormancy. Check on their condition now and then preferably during a mild spell. Any dry, mildew affected leaves should be taken off when the plants are being looked at and the stems sprayed lightly with water to keep them fresh, they should be allowed to dry off again before replacing their protective covering.

Where no building is available for winter storage the dormant plants can often be accommodated in a sheltered spot outside. Choose an out-of-the-way place for this, perhaps an empty border sheltered by a wall – this will be perfect for a wall makes the finest windbreak of all. The fuchsias are plunged quite thickly in the soil and after plants are tidied by reducing the length of the old flowering stems by about a third the process of insulation can begin. Once again use dry bracken leaves or straw to cover the roots, extending the material upwards through the branches until the plants are completely buried. Some fuchsia growers use a low temporary structure with chicken wire to hold the chosen insulating material. Others simply bury the plants in a trench dug in the soil which is filled with leaves, or if the ground is light the soil is used to fill the trench in. Should you choose the latter method do not forget where you buried them when spring comes around! When the worst of the frosts are past is the time to uncover your hibernating stock.

Pruning must now be done, firstly to repair any damage the winter has inflicted, but also to make sure the plant will be sturdy with plenty of vigour. Dead wood is cut back to living tissue, weakly-looking growths are also removed. The laterals are pruned to within two or three leaf nodes of the previous season's growth from the main stems on a typical bush shape, although this does vary according to shape and cultivar. As soon as the prepared site is ready again set them out as before. When a late frost is forecast the tender new shoots can receive the protection of a sheet of newspaper tied lightly in position overnight.

Plants in pots

Pot-grown, the fuchsias are not as a rule very long lived plants – any that have passed their third birthday are often past their best. However, a plant in good heart need not be disposed of at the end of the season. Pot grown specimens that have been used as plants for patio or garden decoration, as summer bedders, or in the greenhouse are overwintered inside in a similar manner to that set out above. They can be kept without any bother where heat is installed but even in a cold house protection is easily effected.

To prepare for dormancy the pots are placed along the pathway of the greenhouse, but instead of the normal generous watering, this is gradually withheld until the plants are fairly dry with most of the foliage having fallen. Do not hurry this process or allow the pots to become dust dry at any time. Plunge the pots to their rims under the staging if the position is suitable, with a thick layer of peat or leaves over the crowns. In a cold house additional covering will be required to make sure that frost does not reach the roots. Pots need not be kept in the light so a cellar or shed will suit just as well. Check on their condition now and again and give a light spray to freshen them up.

Starting up in spring
When cuttings are required for fresh stock, plants are started into growth fairly early in the new year but if there is no urgency it may be left until late spring.

When ready to start, give the pots a thorough soak. Do not attempt the pruning yet but clean the plants by removing all old foliage. One watering should be sufficient to induce the dormant buds to swell, while a gentle spray with tepid water will also help. Only after the buds have started to grow can the pruning and repotting be done. Tackle the pruning first. As all flowers are carried on the current year's growth only, there is little need to keep any more of the old wood than is required to maintain the framework of the plant once the shape has been determined. In practice, most of the shoots produced the previous season are removed by spurring back lateral growths to within two or three buds of the main stems, making the cut to a sprouting bud. At this time it is a good plan to clean old bark from the stems of standards by rubbing gently with a soft nylon brush that has been moistened.

Potting-back is the next job to be tackled. To do this shake out or if preferred carefully wash away as much of the old compost as possible before potting-back using a suitable compost (see p. 27) in a smaller size pot. Water the plant to re-establish it and give shade if the sunshine is very bright until growth starts. The growing cycle of repotting, feeding and stopping can now recommence.

The traditional time for taking cuttings is after growth has started.

7   RAISING NEW STOCK

In previous chapters we have talked only of purchasing plants from a nurseryman. Once a stock has been obtained in this way there is no reason why additional plants should not be raised at home using propagating material from one's own plants or pieces donated by friends. Fortunately for us fuchsias are among the gardening world's more easily increased subjects. Vegetative methods of increasing the stock are essential if the true character of any cultivar or clone is to be retained. Cuttings, usually in a half-ripe state are universally employed for this, as grafting is an art seldom, if ever, employed nowadays. The keen amateur may care to try his hand at grafting as a novelty, although it has very limited practical use for fuchsias.

The third way to increase plants is from seed. It is interesting to experiment in order to see just what will materialise, and most new sorts come about in this way. These are of course the result of careful breeding, many hundreds being discarded before a novelty is considered fit for marketing.

Cuttings

Cuttings will strike readily at any time during the active growing season but the best results are obtained before the wood matures. Half ripe cuttings taken before the summer sun gets too hot will be easier to handle, root quicker and, if taken early enough, will produce a good show of flowers the first season.

In order to produce plants of quality it is essential to select only first class stock. Choose sturdy, straight stems with short spaces between the nodes or leaf joints. Ignore thin shoots or those where the foliage is spaced widely apart, although some cultivars do not grow in a way that is ideal for taking cuttings.

Dormant plants which have been potted back, watered then pruned make fairly rapid growth in early spring. New shoots appearing after the old twigs are spurred back are allowed to grow until they bear some four pairs of leaves together with a plump tip. Remove the selected cutting with a sharp razor blade, leaving two pairs of leaves on the plant from which further shoots will spring. Fuchsias will root from cuttings that are cut between the nodes although most people prefer to cut just below the leaf joint and remove the lower pair of leaves. After removal, these cuttings are inserted into a compost that retains moisture, is sharply drained to remove excess water and is well aerated. J. I. seed with a little extra sand, or a mixture of medium grade sphagnum moss peat and clean sharp river sand in equal proportions will give consistently good results as a substrate or rooting medium. There are many other suitable materials such as moist peat, sand, sandy compost, vermiculite, pumice or even water.

Where only a small quantity of plants is needed, sufficient cuttings can be placed around the edge of a pot; larger numbers are better planted in trays. Label immediately with the name of the cultivar for the memory is remarkably fickle when it comes to trying to remember later. Where a propagating bench complete with intermittent mist is available use it, for fuchsias respond very well to these conditions. Failing this, place pots or boxes of cuttings in a warm part of the greenhouse or frame, keeping the foliage turgid with a light overhead spray when needed. Bottom heat will also be beneficial and rooting will take place remarkably quickly under conditions that are ideal. We have had good results when a polythene bag has been placed over the rim of the pot after the cuttings have been put in. Only one watering is normally enough when this is done, for moisture given off by the foliage is trapped, running back down the inside of the bag into the pot. Also of value when only a few plants are needed and no heating is available are the clear plastic covers that are made to fit both pots and trays; these create just the sort of micro-climate that fuchsias enjoy. When light green tips appear, indicating that the cuttings are rooting, more air must be admitted. It is best to pot on as soon as possible in order that the little plants may not receive a check by remaining too long in a medium that lacks nutrient. J. I. 2 potting compost is our choice for the growing-on period using small pots for the initial move.

Biennial method

Another type of cutting, from which many specimen plants are produced for display the following season, is started from short-jointed, half-ripened shoots taken off the plant for rooting during the summer. Where no greenhouse is available this method will prove a good alternative to striking plants in the spring. Now they can be rooted with the sun's warmth, kept in a sunny window and overwintered before potting on or planting out the following late spring. On many plants it is not easy to find the correct type of shoots to use as all are flowering profusely at this season so

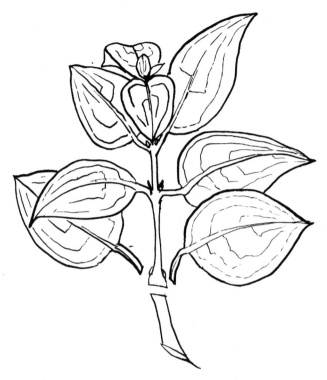

A half-ripe cutting prepared for insertion.

some of the branches should be cut back four weeks before taking cuttings. The cuttings are prepared in a similar way to that described for rooting in the spring (p. 51). After insertion they are watered, then placed in a partly shaded spot in the green-house, frame or even outdoors until rooted. If taken early in the summer they can be potted-on as soon as they have rooted sufficiently, using a free draining compost. This can be standard J. I. 2 or a home-made mixture with a small quantity of a slow release fertiliser added. The first potting in small pots will carry the plants through the winter without further feeding. They should be placed in a light airy place in the greenhouse or by a window. If temperatures are kept slightly above freezing growth will stagnate during the dull days of winter, so keep the compost rather dry but do not allow it to dry out completely. Growth will become more active as the temperatures rise in the spring; at this time a sharp watch must be kept for insects.

The normal potting-on procedure carries on from this point. Where whips are being grown for training as standards do not remove the growing tip but all others can be stopped (see p. 38).

Grafting

Grafting can be employed where a good weeping head of a desired cultivar is wanted on a stout stem. Because of their form many of the best of the cascade type of cultivar do not have the ability to make a straight stem even with careful training. It is sometimes possible to employ a vigorous grower to furnish the trunk (stock) whilst the weaker growing more desirable kind (scion) is grafted in at the required height to form the head. The easiest and most suitable method of grafting fuchsias is to inarch to two plants. This can often be observed in the wild where two branches of a tree have crossed and a natural union takes place as they grow. In the case of the fuchsia, two plants still in their pots are placed adjacently and a sliver of bark is removed from near the top of the standard at the point where the join is to take place. A corresponding piece of bark is cut away from a strong ripe shoot of the plant that is to form the head. The two cut surfaces are brought together quickly and bound with a strip of polythene. Tie this in place but remember to check for tightness as growth commences. When a complete union is judged to have taken place the scion is cut away from the parent. All other growth is now removed from the stock, both below and above the join, so that all the energy is passed entirely to the recipient. The growing shoot must be supported throughout its life if the two halves of the plant are not to part company, for although they are joined with living tissue there is risk of a break owing to the brittle

[54]

growth. Any buds that develop below the union must be rubbed out for they tend to take over the energy of the plant.

Seed

The third way of raising plants is from seed. Although this is the way most new cultivars of fuchsias are raised it does not mean that every seedling that flowers is a winner; in fact more often than not the opposite is true. Deliberate cross pollination is slightly different, for here the hybridist has a definite objective in mind. It may be a new colour, or even a combination of colours but it is more likely to be a plant of better constitution or habit of growth. Even so, many hundreds of seedlings are raised each year only to be discarded as their faults appear. If all this has not put the reader off sowing seeds we will proceed to the method commonly employed.

The seeds are contained in a berry or fleshy capsule which, incidentally, is perfectly edible although rather insipid to the taste. We came across a recipe in an old book for a tart made from fuchsia berries but from the amount of lemon juice required we suspect that this would be the dominant flavour. Most writers advocate squashing the purple or green ripe berries in order to extract the seeds; we find it better to dissect them one at a time using a razor blade. The seeds are scraped out onto a sheet of blotting paper which absorbs most of the water contained with them. Whenever possible, it is best to sow them immediately for then germination is rapid. They are sown in a light, fine, sterilised compost with a minimum covering of silver sand and carefully watered. The pots are shaded with brown paper then placed in a warm place for germination to take place. Check on development now and then, removing the shading as the tiny seed leaves appear. Sown thinly, they can remain in this container in a frost free place until the following spring when potting-off into individual pots is done. Some of the best sorts seem to come from the weaker-looking seedlings so do not discard these until all have flowered. When it is not convenient to sow at once leave the seeds on blotting paper in a sunny place until dry. They are then packeted (together with a record of the cross if it has been deliberate) to be sown the following spring. It is always doubtful whether fuchsia seed will germinate but the best results always come from earlier sowings. Should something appear that seems to be really distinct from any other fuchsias known to the raiser, it is best to check with a specialist before naming. He will have a mental picture of every fuchsia he knows and will be able to advise on the worth of your new plant. When it proves to be distinct from others in cultivation it can receive a name, after propagating. This must be done vegetatively to ensure that the offspring are all identical to the original, as there is little likelihood of their reverting as has sometimes happened when a new plant is raised from a sporting bud. You can call your offspring anything you like providing the name complies with the International Code of Nomenclature for Cultivated Plants and the requirements of the Registration Authority (The American Fuchsia Society). Some of the finest cultivars of fuchsias have been raised by amateurs in the past, so in spite of the rather pessimistic start to this section a pot or two sown to see what comes up may well reward you for your time and patience with something really worth while.

8   PESTS AND DISEASES

The saying 'the best form of defence is attack' might well originally have been coined by a gardener when describing how to deal with glasshouse pests! In the case of the fuchsia this is especially so, for once an infestation is allowed to take hold, although it may be possible to save the plants, the damage already caused may well spoil their decorative effect for the rest of the season. Not that fuchsias are particularly prone to attack for they are comparatively free from such things, particularly the hardy sorts.

Much good will be done when attention is paid conscientiously to the normal cultural requirements of the plant. This means that it is kept growing by repotting, maintaining a moist humid atmosphere and spraying the foliage with water in the early stages of growth. Shade from the hot sun should be provided when needed. In hot dry conditions it is essential that the pathways and staging are kept well damped down, with attention paid to ventilation so as to keep a buoyant circulation of air. Dry air conditions favour the rapid increase of *red spider mite*, a familiar glasshouse pest. Adults over-winter in crevices in the glasshouse structure, staging and brickwork; bamboo canes, straw or other litter also provide shelter. First steps should therefore be towards cleanliness: the walls should be whitewashed or treated with a sterilant such as Jeyes Fluid during the time the house is empty, while fumigation should be done at the same time. The minute eggs hatch under a protective fine web made by the adult female. Newly hatched, the young feed by sucking the sap from the foliage of the fuchsia. Before long, mottled or even dead areas of tissue appear and leaves drop prematurely as a result of the interference with their normal function. Left unchecked the plants will become almost completely defoliated, and will some-times die. A small hand sprayer is one of the best weapons for use in pest control. Filled with water that has had a drop or two of a wetting agent (i.e. soft detergent) added, it is directed towards the underside of the leaves to give them a thorough misting at frequent intervals. This is only partly preventative and is unlikely to lead to complete freedom from attack. When an infestation does occur fumigation or spraying with insecticide will have to be resorted to.

Fumigating a greenhouse is relatively easy these days if smoke cones are used. Read the instructions first. Remove any plants that are known to be prone to damage, close the house, place the cones in position, light those at the far end of the house first and retire immediately. If you are using several and one fails to ignite do not be tempted to re-enter to relight it as this could prove very uncomfortable, to say the least. The operation is best carried out overnight to avoid temperatures rising too high as would happen in a closed house on a hot day. In the morning, ventilate completely before going inside for any length of time. One of the problems of complete control of this pest is the ability of the mites to form an immune strain which shows resistance to the various chemicals used to combat it. Therefore, fumigation is not in itself sufficient to guarantee total kill; in view of this two or more materials should be used in rotation. The old fashioned method of spraying with a soft soap solution is very effective against this pest. Soft soap is not stocked by sundriesmen as much now as formerly, in spite of its value in the garden.

Both this and the next insect pest can be partially controlled by the introduction into the greenhouse of special insect predators, but as these need a constant supply of pests to prey on they can hardly be regarded as a preventative measure. Fairly high temperatures are also needed before they do their stuff so although in theory they sound the perfect way to a pest free glasshouse, to the best of our knowledge they are not entirely successful in practice.

Glasshouse white fly or *ghost fly* as it is sometimes called has always been one of the worst pests to occur on fuchsias, although it infests many other species. Although it sometimes attacks plants growing outdoors in hot dry places which are adjacent to the greenhouse, it is most likely to cause trouble indoors. The green immature young hatch from eggs which are laid in clusters on the lower leaf surface. They crawl about for a short while before settling down to their scale-like stage. The perfect insects emerge from these scales appearing as tiny white moth-like creatures as they flit from plant to plant before settling. They are particularly noticeable when the plants are disturbed. The young feed on the sap, excreting considerable amounts of honeydew in the process. The sticky covering on the foliage breeds *sooty moulds* which although non-parasitic in themselves lead to unsightly fouling of both foliage and flowers. This also upsets the plants' normal respiratory system and results in premature leaf fall. With the *white fly* breeding takes place almost continuously throughout the year whenever temperatures are high enough, with several stages in the life cycle usually present under a leaf once the pest has gained a hold. Control of the adults is relatively easy but the scale-like young often escape because they stay under the leaves so that it is difficult to spray them. If they escape unharmed they will hatch out to continue breeding so that spraying at intervals is essential.

Modern insecticides, fungicides and acaricides (chemicals used for killing mites) can usually be purchased in handy aerosols which make the task of controlling attacks relatively easy. To save on costs small hand pressure sprayers can be used instead

and filled with the dilute chemical as recommended by the manufacturer. Always treat these materials with the respect they
deserve, adhering strictly to the instructions given on the container. Under glass it is not advisable to spray in hot sun or
damage will result, so in warm weather wait until evening before
spraying.

Aphids are plant lice, several different species of which occur on
young tender shoots both indoors and out. Colonies of these
easily identified pests increase very rapidly if left unchecked but
fortunately control is easy if regular attention is paid to the
plants with a small hand sprayer filled with a suitable insecticide.
Honeydew produced by these insects should be sponged from the
foliage with a piece of moist cotton wool.

The waxy coating on the body of the *mealy bug* makes wetting
by a pesticide rather difficult so that a bad attack, although rare,
is most unwelcome. The adult females are wingless but unlike
the young which lead a sedentary existence they can move about.
A dry atmosphere suits this pest and attacks often follow where
the fuchsias are allowed to dry out frequently. Maintaining
humidity will act as a splendid deterrent.

Ants can be blamed for the spread of mealy bugs both inside
and out for they are fond of the honeydew which these pests
secrete. The presence of this sticky substance on the foliage, together with its attendant growth of sooty mould, is often the first
indication of an attack. An aerosol as suggested for aphids is the
remedy. Ants, although not a pest in the usual sense of the word,
cause trouble in two ways: firstly they will take a pot in which to
carry out nest building activities which causes disruption to the
normal growth of the roots. Secondly, as has just been mentioned,
they like honeydew, that sticky substance so liberally secreted by
aphids, white fly and mealy bugs. Ants will move these pests
around to fresh pastures in order to maintain a regular supply.
Insecticide in a powder form dusted in and around pots or plants
where the ants are seen will either kill them or discourage them
from nesting.

Cyclamen mites do not often attack fuchsias but when they do it
is invariably a plant that has suffered from too dry an atmosphere. These conditions are unhappily all too frequent in tiny

glasshouses that are left unattended for many hours each day with the result that ventilation is not correctly carried out. Plants become stunted as a result of the presence of the mites in the roots and the foliage is mottled with rusty patches here and there. To clear up trouble remove the plant from the pot, shake off as much soil as possible and finally soak the roots in a mild insecticide for a few minutes. The plant can now be repotted in fresh compost and shaded for a day or two with frequent syringing of the foliage.

The *capsid bug* is a bright green insect that resembles a large slender aphid and which causes damage on fuchsias growing outside, although on occasion it will visit plants growing in greenhouses too. They have two distinct stages in their life cycle. The adult females lay their eggs on certain woody plants in the autumn; these hatch in the spring, soon becoming very active at feeding on the sap of the soft young shoots of the host plant. When partly grown they migrate by crawling to new plants – this is where the fuchsia is likely to be involved. Damage is caused by the bug's injecting a toxic substance into the leaf on which it is feeding. To the capsid bug this saliva is only an aid to digestion but the plant cells react strongly to it by curling their leaves; the stems twist and curl with the flower buds often too distorted to open correctly. The normal method of control is to spray with a tar oil winter wash. This is fine on fruit trees and other hosts but of little use to fuchsia growers as the bugs are not present on fuchsias in winter. It is in the crawling stage that we have to counter them. Frequent spraying in early summer using the suggested insecticide (see chart, p. 195) will hopefully keep them in check.

An attack by *thrips* is another likely result of growing plants in adverse conditions. Bright light and dry air encourage these tiny black insects but it is the nymphs, as the young are called, that do the most damage. They hatch from minute eggs laid on the under leaf surfaces, feeding in colonies between the ribs of the leaf which becomes discoloured from their continual sucking of the sap. In a bad attack the whole of the under leaf surfaces are covered with a sticky black secretion which will ruin the plant if left unchecked. Control is by spraying.

When in the larval stage the *vine weevil* will feed on the roots of pot grown plants making the leaves turn yellow and wilt in hot weather. It is not easy to control without removing all the soil from the root ball; the white grubs with brown heads will be seen when it is shaken off. The roots of the plant are soaked for a few moments in a mild solution of suitable insecticide before repotting in fresh compost. Adult vine weevil feed at night eating out small pieces of foliage but in general are not as troublesome on fuchsias as on other plants such as ferns, *Primula* or saxifrage.

Caterpillars of various species of moth can sometimes be found chewing foliage. Pick these off as soon as seen.

Bees of different species can damage flowers and also by fertilising them whilst in search of nectar cause the flowers to fall immediately they mature. *Wasps* often eat large chunks of the flower. The only remedy is to provide ventilators and a door with netting of sufficiently small mesh to prevent their entry. *Leaf cutter bees* will on occasion trim neat pieces from leaves to use in nest building. This is unfortunate if the specimen is destined for a show but otherwise best ignored.

Diseases

Fuchsia rust is sometimes recorded on fuchsias growing in greenhouses. Orange-yellow eruptions mostly occur on the under leaf surface, although in a bad attack the whole leaf will be covered. As the wild willow herb is frequently attacked, steps should be taken to ensure that it is eradicated from anywhere near the vicinity of the greenhouse. In the event of the disease's affecting a fuchsia any foliage showing the symptoms must be removed from the plant before it falls, then burned to stop the spread of the fungus. As soon as the disease is suspected spray the plants with a fungicide at intervals until it is entirely cleared up.

Grey mould (Botrytis cinerea) occurs when a dank or humid, stuffy atmosphere persists. It can appear at any time of the year, young plants in winter being particularly prone to attack. All infected leaves should be picked off, for where they lie across a stem this will very often rot too. Maintaining a free flow of air usually clears up serious trouble; if not the house should be fumigated. Grey mould also affects plants growing outdoors when

[61]

it rots flowers and foliage alike but fortunately this is almost always at the end of the season. When it happens try to allow the plants' foliage to dry off completely before bringing them inside. A dusting with a fungicide will help control the spread of the disease.

Yet another fungus disease to be on the look out for is *black root* (*Thielaviopsis basicola*) which is sometimes called *root-rot* for that is what it does. This soil- or water-borne fungus is normally encountered only in unsterilised compost, so we think it worth the effort to see that loam is treated before it is incorporated in potting materials. Roots turn black and rot as the fungus invades the cells which leads to a severe restriction in the growth of the plant. Foliage does not usually fall as might be expected but does wilt very easily as soon as the temperature rises. There are two methods of dealing with this trouble. The use of a systemic fungicide should be sufficient to control a mild attack but when the attack is severe the plant must be removed from its pot, the compost removed, the dead roots cut away and the plant must be repotted in fresh sterilised compost. You should water with a mild fungicide two or three times at intervals of two weeks or so.

Not all problems are caused by pests and diseases. Physiological disorders, as they have been termed, can be brought about by great fluctuations in the temperature as when, for instance, plants are brought straight from a heated greenhouse to much cooler conditions outside. When fuchsias have not been hardened off sufficiently the foliage will probably turn dark purple within a day or so but although the plant has had a great shock it will usually make a good recovery when the new shoots appear. This will curtail the flowering for a time so it is far better to go to the trouble of seeing that hardening is done in stages.

Damage can also be brought about by the over-generous use of fertilisers; the roots suffer when this happens but the first signs are yellow or blotchy leaves with dark green veining. When only slightly affected the mere fact that the feeding is discontinued is normally enough to allow the plant to make a complete recovery. Should it still look anaemic after some weeks re-pot it into fresh compost.

Chemical sprays can cause severe scorching to tender foliage especially on some cultivars. As a precaution against this use only recommended materials at the correct strength. Spotting of foliage can also come about when plants are watered or remain wet in a sunny greenhouse, so see that they are watered in the late evening or early morning.

Pest control chart (see page 196)
From the pest control chart it will be seen that two methods (spraying and fumigating) will control most of the insects likely to be encountered in growing fuchsias. In practice either an aerosol or a small hand sprayer filled with a suitable insecticide (alone or in mixture) will be the most commonly used. Do not wait for an attack of aphids or white fly to occur before spraying but make up a small quantity every two weeks and go over the plants paying particular attention to the under leaf surfaces and growing tips.

Some troubles are not cured with the use of a sprayer but will need a fumigant or smoke cone which when lit sends off a dense cloud of insecticide filled smoke to permeate every part of the greenhouse structure. These can also be used as a preventative rather than cure.

THE COLOUR PLATES

1.   'Melody'

2. 'Carmen'

3. 'Lena Dalton'

4. 'Royal Touch'

5. 'Mandarin'

6. 'Texas Longhorn'

7. 'Blush of Dawn' 8. 'Centerpiece'

9. 'Pat Meara' 10. 'Rigoletto'

11. 'Bernadette'

12. 'Flirtation Waltz'

13. 'Whirlaway'

14.   'Madame Van der Strass'

15. 'Coachman'

16. 'Checkerboard'

17. 'Mrs Lovell Swisher'

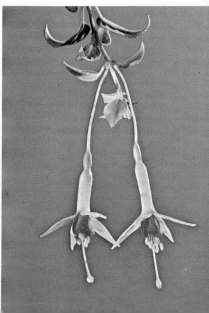

18. 'David Lockyer'

19. 'Voltaire'

20. 'Lollypop'

21. 'Rose of Castile, Improved'

22. 'La Fiesta'

23. 'Strawberry Delight'

24. 'Sierra Blue'

25. 'Blue Waves'

26. 'Impudence'

27.   'Phénoménal'

28. 'Joan Cooper'

29. 'Pee Wee Rose'

30. 'Red Spider'

31. 'Falling Stars'

32. 'Curly Q'

33. 'Forget-me-Not'   34. 'Dorothea Flower'

35. 'Mr A. Huggett'

36. 'Balkon'

37. 'Bonnie Lass'

38. 'Pink Darling'

39. 'Alyce Larson'

40. 'Graf Witte'

41. 'White Pixie'

42. 'Chillerton Beauty' (outdoors)

43. 'Chillerton Beauty' (inside)

44. *F. magellanica* 'Tricolor'

45. 'Tom Thumb'

46. 'Flash'

47. *F. magellanica* 'Gracilis'

48. 'Abbé Farges'

49. 'Phyllis'

50. 'Pink Pearl'

51. 'Empress of Prussia'

52. 'Major Heaphy'

53. 'Royal Purple'

54. 'Swanley Yellow'

55. 'Lye's Unique'

56. 'Crackerjack'

57. 'Jack Shahan'

58. 'Fiona'

59. 'Cascade'

60. 'Pink Galore'

61. 'Swanley Gem'

62. 'Flashlight'

63. 'Lady Isobel Barnett'

64. 'Joy Patmore'

65. 'Kwintet'

66.   'Heidi Ann'   67.   'White Ann' (inset)

68. 'King's Ransom'

69. 'Lovable'

70. 'Dutch Mill'

71. 'Red Ribbons'

72.   'Cloth of Gold'

73.   'Margery Blake'

74.   'Army Nurse', 'Sunray'

75.   'Golden Marinka'

76.   'Winston Churchill'

77. 'Lena'

78. 'Morning Light'

79. 'Tiffany'

80. 'Cotton Candy'

81. 'Pathétique'

82. 'Kon Tiki'

83. 'Regal Robe'

84. 'Lilac Lustre'

85.   'Danny Boy'

86. 'Collingwood'

87. 'San Diego'

88. 'Granada'

89. 'Sleigh Bells'

90.   'Sonata'

91. 'Marin Glow'

92. 'Countess of Aberdeen'

93. 'Rufus'

94. 'Diana Wills'

95. 'Beauty of Bath'

96. 'Strawberry Sundae'

97. 'Sweet Sixteen'

98. 'Indian Maid'

99. 'Charlie Girl'

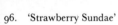

100. 'Miss California'

101. 'Lilian Lampard'   102. 'Tranquility'

103. 'Raspberry'

104. 'Leibriez'
105. 'Princess Dollar'

106. 'Pink Bon Accorde'

107. 'Caesar'

108. 'Melody'   109. 'Ting-a-Ling'

110. 'Louise Emershaw'   111. 'Keystone'

112. 'Pepi'

113. 'Minnesota'   114. 'Rose of Castile'

115. 'Leonora'

116. 'Tristesse' 117. 'Alice Hoffman'

118. 'Queen Mary' 119. 'Henriette Ernst'

120. 'Golden Dawn'

121. 'White Spider'

122. 'Lord Lonsdale'

123. 'Alaska'

124. 'Andrew'

125. 'Ambassador'

126. 'Chang'

127. 'Kolding Perle'

128. 'Marinka'

129. 'The Doctor'

130. 'Dilly Dilly'

131. 'Gay Fandango'

132. 'Tolling Bell'

133. 'Lord Roberts'

134. 'Gruss aus dem Bodethal'

135. 'Orange Flare'

136. 'Mieke Meursing'

137. *F. arborescens*

138. 'Trailing Queen'   139. 'Caledonia'

140. *F. boliviana* var. *luxurians*

141. *F. boliviana* var. *luxurians* 'Alba'

142. 'Arthur Cope'

143. 'Mrs Churchill'

144. 'Pink Fairy'

145. 'Flair'

146. 'R.A.F.'

147. 'Lucky Strike'   148. 'Lyric'

149. 'Personality'   150. 'Peppermint Stick'

151. 'Swingtime'

152. 'Charming'

53. 'Otherfellow'

154. 'Comet'

155. 'Sophisticated Lady'

156. 'Sarong'

157. 'Shooting Star'

158. 'Midnight Sun'   159. 'White Fairy'

160. 'Fancy Pants'   161. 'Caroline'

162. 'Prelude'

163. "New Fascination"

164. 'Sweet Leilani'

165. 'Shady Blue'

166.   'Snowcap'

167. 'Brutus'

168. 'Treasure'

169. 'Bon Bon'

170. 'Constellation'

171. 'Rhapsody'

172. 'Flying Cloud'   173. 'Ruffles'

174. 'Television'   175. 'Ziegfield Girl'

176. 'Mary'   177. 'Trumpeter'

178. 'Coralle'

179. 'Hindu Belle'   180. 'Trail Blazer'

181. 'Traudchen Bonstedt'

182. 'Thalia'

183. 'Torch'

184. 'Billy Green'

185. 'Susan Ford'

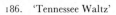

186. 'Tennessee Waltz'

187. 'La Neige'

188. 'Port Arthur'

189. 'Alison Ryle'

190.   'Arabella'

191. 'Spring Bells'

192. 'Cosmopolitan'

193. 'Symphony'

194. 'Muriel'

195. 'Dainty Lady'   196. 'Laura'

197. 'Tahoe'   198. 'Temptation'

199. 'Spotlight'

DESCRIPTIONS

In the notes which follow only the briefest remark about each cultivar has been possible owing to the number involved. It has not been the intention to include here all the plants at present in cultivation around the world or offered for sale by nurserymen but only a good selection of the more popular sorts. Cultivation notes have, where possible, been based on our own experience except for some new plants for which we have relied on the notes furnished by other growers. Growing conditions vary from country to country, and this is nowhere more apparent than when discussing the subject of hardiness. Plants marked in the list as hardy can remain outside as permanent planting in cold countries such as Britain where they will form a valuable addition to the range of summer and autumn flowering shrubs. In warm countries not subject to cold winters, the often more showy, tender sorts can remain outside or in a shade house for the whole twelve months.

Flower colour or even habit of growth can alter according to climate, cultivation and the amount of sun received so the colours mentioned must only be taken as a rough guide. The raiser or the firm introducing a new plant to cultivation and the date on which this was done will very often be a guide to the correct name for a given plant. When known it has been included in the description, next to the name. Our apologies in advance if any mistakes have occurred.

Not all fuchsias have the same natural habit of growth and if left to their own devices many will sprawl about in an ungainly manner so, except for the hardy cultivars, nearly all will be better if some form of training is carried out when the plant is immature. Most can be used as bush plants, grown in the ground or pots but natural upright growers will be the easiest to form into standards or trees. Stiff branches are a help when it comes to creating a pyramid shape. Vigorous growers make good climbers. Upright, bushy forms are valued for planting out, for the blooms are held well up from the soil so they do not get damaged from being splashed in bad weather. Several of the more spectacular of the

American cultivars are called trailers: their stems instead of growing upwards tend to grow sideways and down. These need initial pinching out to make several breaks if a bush form is desired. The next step is some form of support – several thin canes are best for a bush. The more vigorous of the trailers will make good standards or trees if allowed to grow unstopped and secured to a single stout cane. Plants with slender stems can be used for baskets but the best of all for this purpose are those in the cascade group, grown in an elevated pot or basket, with the stems allowed to trail down in a natural manner. (See p. 38 for more details of initial shaping.)

'Abbé Farges' (48) LEMOINE 1901 French
Calyx crimson. Corolla – semi-double, lavender then rose-lilac. Small flowers profusely carried on this upright plant of good form.

'Achievement' MELVILLE 1876 British
Calyx – clear red. Corolla – single, rose-purple. Individual flowers are large and of attractive form. Standard.

'Aileen' SOO YUN 1972 American
Tube – short, light green; sepals – cream with green tips. Corolla – double, cerise, paling at base of petals. The medium size flowers are freely produced. Plant is bushy and upright.

'Alaska' (123) SCHNABEL 1963 American
Rounded, well-filled double white flowers with the reverse of the petals lightly tinged in pink. Vigorous grower, rather more spreading than upright.

'Alfred Rambaud' LEMOINE 1896 French
Calyx – dark red. Corolla – double, deep violet then purple-violet. Bushy.

'Alice Hoffman' (117) KLEISE 1911 German
Calyx – rose-pink. Corolla – semi-double, white, fine red veins. Hardy. Neat habit of growth which branches well. Dwarf, to 18 in.

'Alison Ryle' (189) RYLE 1968 British
Calyx – bright cerise. Corolla – semi-double, deep blue then rose-lavender, distinct red veins. This excellent large-flowered plant for garden or greenhouse was a seedling from 'Tennessee Waltz'.

'Alyce Larson' (39) TIRET 1972 American
Tube – white; sepals – pink, recurved. Corolla – double, pure white. Thin wiry growth makes this a natural for use as a trailer in a large basket.

'Ambassador' (125) JONES 1960 British
Calyx – white then pink, sepals – deeper pink inside. Corolla – single, deep violet then purple. There is a marked difference between the newly opened flower and one that has matured which gives the plant a distinctive appearance. Vigorous, upright.

'Americana Elegans' pre 1932
Calyx – red. Corolla single, purple. Flowers are slender, small and of *F. magellanica* type. Hardy. Upright grower with new growth springing from below the soil. Will prove suitable for making a hedge.

[147]

'Amy Lye' LYE 1885(?) British
Calyx – cream with wax-like appearance, under sepals pink. Corolla – single, orange-red. Pleasing bronze new foliage against which the two-tone blooms display well. Upright or basket.

'Andenken an Heinrich Henkel' ('**H. Henkel**') REHNELT 1902 German
Calyx – rose, wax-like, of long tubular *triphylla* type. Corolla – single, salmon. Foliage dark reddish green. Bush.

'Andrew' (**124**) WATSON 1967 British
Tube – cream; sepals – rose-madder. Corolla – single, purple then rose-purple. Upright, bush.

'Angela Leslie' TIRET 1959 American
Calyx – pale pink, sepals recurving. Corolla – double, clear pink spotted and veined deep rose, very full. Free flowering and spectacular under ideal cool conditions in the greenhouse.

'Angel's Flight' MARTIN 1957 American
Tube – white, long; sepals – pink, wide. Corolla – double, white. The sepals are turned upwards and before curling around extend the whole length of the tube. Stamens are clear pink which contrast well with the open, full corolla. Basket.

'Aquarius' SOO YUN 1971 American
Calyx – light pink, sepals deeper on underside. Corolla – single, pink, bell-shaped of medium size. Dark green leaves have serrated edges. Upright or basket.

F. arborescens var. arborescens (**137**) Central America (Section Schufia)
Flowers – rose-lilac (including pedicels), small, in erect terminal corymb-like panicles, similar in appearance to the flowers of 'Lilac' (*syringa*) which has given rise to the synonym *Fuchsia syringaeflora* and a common name, Lilac fuchsia. A small tree which reaches 26 ft (8 m) in the wild, it is normally treated as a large bushy shrub in the greenhouse. The attractive foliage is large and elliptic, narrowed to each end. The plant has a reputation for being slightly hardy but this is probably in the very mildest part of the British Isles.

'Arabella' (**190**) BANKS 1865 British
Calyx – creamy-white, wax-like. Corolla – single, deep carmine-rose. Flowers are carried in clusters. Cascade.

'Army Nurse' (74) HODGES 1947 American

Fairly hardy, this cultivar bears a profusion of small semi-double carmine and violet blooms. Upright in growth, it makes a good standard or pyramid when grown with protection.

'Arthur Cope' (142) GADSBY 1971 British

Calyx – white, long tube and wide sepals. Corolla – single or semi-double, spiraea red flushed with rose, with white at the base of petals. Vigorous, spreading growth.

'Athela' WHITEMAN 1942 British

Tube – cream; sepals – pink. Corolla – single, salmon. A plant of sturdy, clean, good looks with 'Rolla' and 'Mrs Rundle' as its parents.

'Australia Fair' RAWLINS 1954 British

Calyx – bright red. Corolla – double, white with pink flush and red veins. Smallish flowers produced in quantity. Will bed out for the summer in a sheltered spot. Upright, bushy.

x bacillaris Mexico and garden hybrid (Section Encliandra)

Almost all of the Encliandra section in cultivation are derived from this hybrid between *F. microphylla* and *F. thymifolia*. A typical plant has small leaves and a profusion of tiny flowers which are carried singly in the leaf axils. Colour varies from white to coral red. Fairly hardy, can be planted on a rock garden where although cut back by frost they will grow again to make a bright show during summer and autumn. With protection can grow very tall.

'Balkon' ('Balkonkonigen') (36) NEUBRONNER about 1890 German

Tube – white to pale pink; sepals – pale flesh pink deeper on inside. Corolla – single, rose-red. Tiny flowers in bunches. Thin trailing growth. Basket.

'Ballet Girl' VEITCH 1894 British

Calyx – red. Corolla – double, white, long, thin red veins. Large flowers of good substance make this one of the best of the many 'red and whites'.

'Bella Forbes' FORBES 1890 British

Calyx – bright cerise. Corolla – double, creamy-white, very full opening out well. The unmistakable bronze young foliage adds to the beauty of the plant.

'Bellbottoms' CASTRO 1972 American
Tube – salmon; sepals – pale orange, long and thin curling back. Corolla – single, purple with reddish flush to base of petals. On maturing the distinct bell-shape of the corolla assumes a 'smoky-orange' hue. Upright grower.

'Bernadette' (11) SCHNABEL 1950 American
Calyx – rose with green tips to sepals. Corolla – double, veronica-blue then mauve, petals delightfully waved. Stiff branches rather more upright than spreading. Small dark green foliage.

'Beauty of Bath' (95) COLVILLE 1965 British
Calyx – pale pink, long sepals. Corolla – semi-double, white, oval. Upright, bush.

'Billy Green' (184) RAWLINS 1966 British
Flowers – single, pale salmon-pink of *triphylla* form, produced in clusters. Fresh olive-green foliage. This strong grower is a most popular 'show' plant. Bush.

'Bishop's Bells' GADSBY 1970 British
Calyx – crimson, short tube, broad sepals. Corolla – single or semi-double, petunia-purple, bell shaped. Very large flowers that are, according to the raiser, at their best in partial shade. Upright, vigorous.

'Bland's New Striped' BLAND 1872 British
Calyx – bright cerise, sepals partially recurve and twist. Corolla – double, rich purple with ragged streaks of rose to each petal. A flower of distinctive appearance.

'Blue Bush' GADSBY 1974 British
Calyx – rose-red with sepals held well out. Corolla – single, 'Bluebird' blue then pale bishops violet. Hardy. Strong grower.

'Blue Butterfly' WALTZ 1960 American
Calyx – white, short tube and long, slender sepals. Corolla – semi-double, deep violet-blue with white marbling. The corolla opens wide when mature to show the colour change for then the petals are pink with blue markings. Trailing willowy stems with small dark green foliage.

'Blue Lagoon' TIRET 1961 American
Calyx – rose-red. Corolla – double, blue with darker blue veining, very large blooms.

'Blue Mist' TIRET 1964 American

Calyx – rose-pink. Corolla – double, blue with heavy pink markings.

'Blue Pearl' MARTIN 1955 American
Calyx – clear pink, the broad arching sepals have green tips. Corolla – double, violet-blue. Vigorous upright or trailing depending on method of training.

'Blue Petticoat' EVANS–REEVES 1954 American
Calyx – white, rose blush to underside of sepals. Corolla – lavender then orchid-pink. The medium sized flowers are a charming mixture of pastel shades.

'Blue Pinwheel' STUBBS 1970 American
Calyx – bright red, long sepals spread outwards in pinwheel fashion. Corolla – single, blue then pink, petals in the form of a tube. Small dark foliage. Trailing.

'Blue Sleigh Bells' BARTON 1970 New Zealand
Calyx – white, sepals curling back. Corolla – single, lavender-blue, bell-shaped. An upright growing plant of dainty appearance.

'Blue Waves' (25) WALTZ 1954 American
Tube – pink, rather short; sepals – rose, upturned. Corolla – double, deep violet-blue with blue markings. Outer petals of corolla marbled pink. Flower matures with a waved, open centre – an apt name. Sturdy, free flowering.

'Blush of Dawn' (7) MARTIN 1962 American
Calyx – cream, 'dawn' pink on the reverse of each sepal, deeper pink inside. Corolla – double, pale lavender then silver-blue. An unusual colour that makes a good contrast with the deeper shades in a collection. Trailer.

'Boerhave' VAN WIERINGEN 1970 Netherlands
Calyx – deep red. Corolla – single, dark rose-red, extremely long blooms.

F. boliviana West Indies, Central and South America (Section Eufuchsia)
Flowers up to 3 in. in length, deep crimson tube and sepals, corolla slightly paler, borne in drooping panicle-like clusters. Foliage is large, rather soft, elliptic with toothed margins. Forms a branching shrub, most spectacular when flowering.

var. luxurians (140) The form in cultivation. *F. corymbiflora* which is sometimes seen listed, although bearing the name of a true species is almost certainly another version of *F.*

boliviana var. *luxurians*.

var. luxurians 'Alba' (141)
Often seen as *F. corymbiflora
alba*, this magnificent plant has
very long flowers with the white
tube contrasting starkly with
the small, blood red corolla.

'Bon Accorde' CROUSSE French
Calyx – white. Corolla –
single, pale purple. Flowers,
which face upwards, are profusely borne. Plant tends to get
top-heavy when grown naturally as a bush so pinch well in
early stages of growth or take
advantage of upright habit to
make an attractive half-
standard.

'Bon Bon' (169) KENNETT 1963
American
Tube – greenish-white, very
long; sepals – pale rose. Corolla – double, pale pink. Graceful with long stems that arch
when flowers are out.

'Bonnie Lass' (37) WALTZ
1962 American
Calyx – 'frosty-white' with
green tips to sepals. Corolla –
single, clear lilac becoming
rose. Flowers smallish and of
exquisite form. Foliage is small,
dark green. Loose bush, upright.

'Bountiful' MUNKNER 1963
American
Tube – white; sepals – pale
pink with green tips, deeper

pink on the underside. Corolla –
double, white with pink veins.
Free-growing plant with large
'bountiful' flowers.

'Bouquet' ROZAIN-BOUCHAR-
LAT 1893 French
An *F. magellanica* hybrid with
red and violet-purple double
flowers. Hardy, dwarf, bushy.

'Bridesmaid' TIRET 1952
American
Calyx – white with pink flush
more pronounced on the
underside of the wide recurving
sepals. Corolla – double, pale
lilac deepening on the outer
petals. Flowers of good substance on a strong, bushy,
upright plant.

'Brigadoon' ERICKSON 1957
American
Calyx – pink with green tips to
the long, broad, recurved
sepals. Corolla – double, violet-
blue overlaid and marbled at
base of petals with fuchsine-
pink. Long buds open into
large flowers carried on thin
willowy branches. Basket.

'Brilliant' BULL 1865 British
Calyx – red with recurved
sepals. Corolla – single, violet
then magenta. Flowers of good
size, rather long. Very vigorous
plant that makes a fine standard.

'Brutus' (167) LEMOINE 1897
French

Calyx – bright red. Corolla – single, dark purple, almost black, then purple with red veins. Strong bushy grower, another good subject to form into a standard.

'Caballero' KENNETT 1965 American

Calyx – salmon-pink. Corolla – double, purple then magenta with salmon-pink markings on outer petals. The large fully double flower is further enhanced by red or white petaloids. This bushy plant is often treated as a trailer.

'Caesar' (107) FUCHSIA FOREST 1967 American

Calyx – red. Corolla – double, rich purple becoming reddish-purple with red overtones to some petals. Continuous flowering with massive blooms that will certainly need supporting. Upright or trailer.

'Caledonia' (139) LEMOINE 1899 French

Calyx – cerise. Corolla – violet then reddish purple. Hardy with tiny flowers in abundance. Upright and wide spreading.

'Candlelight' WALTZ 1959 American

Calyx – white, slight flush to the underside of the broad upturned sepals. Corolla – double, purple-lilac with rose base to many petals. On ma-turing the corolla is bright carmine. Upright and bushy.

'Carmen' LEMOINE 1893 French

Another old cv still grown, of the red and purple group. This one has a lot of *F. magellanica* about it and bears single or semi-double flowers. Dwarf and hardy, it is suitable for the rockery.

'Carmen' (2) BLACKWELL British

Calyx – bright red with sepals that reflex right back. Corolla – double, campanula blue and pink then clear magenta. Trailer. Like all fuchsias of John Blackwell's raising the name of this one has a musical connection.

'Carnival' TIRET 1959 American

Tube – white or pink; sepals – white with green tips and sides. Corolla – double, bright red. Very distinct flower not only in colour but also in form with the sepals rolled right back to reveal the brilliant colouring of the petals.

'Caroline' (161) MILLER 1967 British

Calyx – cream with pink flush, large sepals held upwards. Corolla – single, lavender then pink. Wide open, large flowers. A beautiful cv that always attracts attention. Upright, vigorous.

'Cascade' (59) LAGEN 1937 British
Calyx – white with pink flush. Corolla – single, rich carmine. Very free flowering, true to its name this plant will provide a wealth of cascading flowers when grown in a pot or basket.

'Celia Smedley' ROE 1970 British
Tube – pale green; sepals – white with pink blush, slightly recurved. Corolla – single although it will at times produce a semi, bright red. Upright, lustrous green foliage. Recommended as a summer bedding out plant.

'Centerpiece' (8) FUCHSIA FOREST 1964 American
Calyx – bright red. Corolla – semi-double, lavender-blue with pink outer petals which spread out to form a large flower as the bloom matures. Said originally to be an upright, but ours always trails!

'Chang' (126) HAZARD 1946 American
Calyx – orange-red with a hint of cerise. Corolla – single, bright orange. Small flowers of brilliant colouration. Large leaves, soft to the touch. An easy grower in a warm position outside (summer only in

Britain) or in a light, bright greenhouse. 'Baby Chang' is a smaller edition.

'Charlie Girl' (99) TANFIELD 1970 British
Calyx – rose-pink with sepals that curve upwards. Corolla – double, lilac-blue veined with deep rose. A strong grower with solid blooms of good form. Upright.

'Charming' (152) LYE 1895 British
A charming red and light purple single, flowers in quantities, weatherproof. Hardy, bushy self-branching. Try it as a greenhouse standard.

'Checkerboard' (16) WALKER-JONES 1948 American
Tube – bright cerise; sepals red and white. Corolla – single, deep red. The long-tubed flowers are carried on very long pedicels and although not large by some standards the plant is most striking, especially when trained so that the flowers are at eye-level. Upright, stiff growth.

'Chillerton Beauty' (42, 43) BASS 1847 British
Calyx – white with rose edged sepals. Corolla – single, violet then mauve, small flowers. Hardy, prolific. Will grow in a greenhouse but there is far better colour in the garden

plants.

'China Doll' WALKER-JONES 1950 American
Calyx – red, the sepals are held downwards. Corolla – double, white, wide-flaring petals. Trailing form.

'China Lantern' American
Tube – deep pink; sepals – white tipped with green. Corolla – single, rose-vermilion paling towards the base of petals. Very attractive flower colour. Upright grower although it tends to become straggly.

'Circe' KENNETT 1965 American
Calyx – pale pink. Corolla – semi-double, centre petals are pale blue then lilac, outer petals pink. The large corolla opens out almost flat. Upright.

'Citation' HODGES 1953 American
Calyx – rose-pink; sepals reflex. Corolla – single, white with pink veins radiating from the base of each petal. The four petals open right out. An interesting form, free flowering, bushy, upright.

'Cliff's Hardy' GADSBY 1970 British
Calyx – crimson with extra thick sepals. Corolla – single, campanula violet, small flowers. Hardy, bushy. A nice little plant raised by one of the most well known of the British raisers, Cliff Gadsby.

'Cloth of Gold' (**72**) STAFFORD 1863 British
Golden foliage with green margins to leaves, the young growth has bronze tones. Small red and purple flowers. Vigorous, best in a sunny place (outside in the summer). A very old cv of which there seem to be several distinct clones. This was a sport of an even older plant 'Souvenir de Chiswick' raised in 1855.

'Cloverdale' GADSBY 1972 British
Calyx – crimson with short, thin tube. Corolla – cornflower blue then purple. Good as a pot or show plant with small single flowers on a well-formed mini bush.

'Cloverdale Jewel' GADSBY 1974 British
Calyx – bright rose. Corolla – single, wistaria blue. Free flowering neat grower with flowers held away from the foliage.

'Coachman' (**15**) BRIGHT about 1920 British
Calyx – pale salmon, long tube. Corolla – single, deep red. Flowers in clusters. Attractive pale green, soft foliage. Vigorous with thick stems.

Will quickly make a standard.

'Collingwood' (86) NEIDER-HOLZER 1945 American
Calyx – soft pink, sepals turned back. Corolla – double, white with pink veins. Foliage is a shining deep green against which the large flowers of delicate colouring are shown to perfection.

'Comet' (154) TIRET 1963 American
Calyx – red. Corolla – double, magenta. Upright but stems bend down with the weight of the many brightly coloured blooms.

'Constance' BERKELEY HORTI-CULTURAL NURSERY 1935 American
Resembles 'Pink Pearl' (from which it was a sport) except for the colour of the corolla. Instead of rose as in the parent this one is blue-mauve tinted pink, double.

'Constellation' (170) SCHNA-BEL 1957 American
Calyx – pure white, long pointed sepals. Corolla – double, creamy white. Flowers of moderate size displayed against small dark foliage. Bushy growth with thin stems which arch downwards unless staked.

'Coralle' ('Koralle') (178) BONSTEDT 1905 German

Rich orange flowers of tubular, *triphylla* type carried in clusters which get longer and larger as the season progresses. Dark green foliage with slight 'bloom'.

'Cordifolia' Garden origin
Flowers red and green, solitary in the upper leaf-axils. The calyx is downy, tube dull red with the green sepals tinged red along their edges. The petals of the corolla are pale green or yellowish-white. Foliage is smooth, toothed, opposite. A tall growing, warm greenhouse subject of interest to the collector. Although it bears the name of a true species the plant grown is of garden origin, presumably a hybrid.

'Corsair' KENNETT 1965 American
Calyx – white. Corolla – double, opens sky-blue then changes to light purple. Base of each petal is white with distinct white lines extending over most of the petal. The outer petals are white and bear purple markings. Heavy blooms on a plant that can be used as a bush or trailer.

'Cosmopolitan' (192) FUCHSIA FOREST 1960 American
Calyx – red, thick sepals. Corolla – double, pink and white, outer petals coral, these

twist and curl – most effective. Bush or will trail.

'Cotton Candy' (80) TIRET 1962 American
Calyx – white, the sepals curl right back to display the very full corolla. Corolla – double, pale pink. Upright grower with large, thick dark green foliage. Upright, bush.

'Countess of Aberdeen' (92) DOBBIE-FORBES 1888 British
Calyx – cream, white or pink depending on the amount of sun where the plant is growing. Corolla – single, soft pink. Small flowers, light green foliage. Bushy, upright growth. Appears to have much *F. magellanica* var. *molinae* in its ancestry.

'Crackerjack' (56) FUCHSIALA 1961 American
Calyx – white with hint of pink, sepals long, narrow. Corolla – single or semi-double, pale blue then mauve. The pedicels are very long and thin giving the flower a delicate appearance. The plant however is of robust constitution although of a trailing nature. Basket.

Crimson Bedder' pre 1889 British
An old coloured foliage plant of great charm. Leaves of crimson and bronze are margined in white. The small flowers of red and purple are of secondary importance for it is the brightly coloured leaves that are the feature. An Australian nurseryman suggests planting in a basket for effect.

'Crinoline' REITER 1950 American
Calyx – white; the sepals have green tips. Corolla – double, rose-pink. Upright, sturdy grower.

'Curly Q' (32) KENNETT 1961 American
Calyx – cream, carmine stripes; the sepals roll right up into little circles which lie against the tube. Corolla – single, violet-purple. Charming small flowers, unusual greyish foliage and an easy plant to shape.

'Curtain Call' MUNKNER 1961 American
Calyx – cream flushed rose. Corolla – double, deep rose paler toward the centre. The petals have distinctly serrated edges. Large flowers. Bush or will trail.

'Dainty Lady' (195) LOWE British
Calyx – bright red. Corolla – semi-double, white with clear red veins. The flowers in which the wide sepals reflex straight up are displayed well against the dark green foliage. Bush.

'Danny Boy' (85) TIRET 1961 American
Tube – white; sepals – magenta flush, darker on underside. Corolla – double, dark plum-red. Very large blooms. Strong, upright grower.

'David Alston' FORBES 1906 British
Large double flowers with red calyx and white, suffused pink corolla.

'David Lockyer' (18) HOLMES 1968 British
Calyx – white. Corolla – double, dark and light red with white stripes. A very large flower, of a size that is usually associated with the American raisers. Tall grower.

'Derby Belle' GADSBY 1970 British
Calyx – white with rose flush. Corolla – single, violet-magenta, open, bell-shaped. An attractive plant of easy culture.

'Derby Imp' GADSBY 1974 British
Calyx – crimson. Corolla – single, violet-blue. Flowers are small, early. Dwarf, free-branching growth.

'Diablo' TIRET 1961 American
Calyx – white. Corolla – double, burgundy-red. Large, flowers. Trailer or bush.

'Diana Wills' (94) GADSBY 1971 British

Calyx – white, wax-like with green-tipped sepals. Corolla – double, purple-red with rose markings then ruby-red. Large commanding flowers. Bushy, upright.

'Display' SMITH 1881 British
Calyx – deep rose-red. Corolla – single, deep cerise, petals arranged as an open cup. The colours of the flower blend so that from a distance they appear to be self-coloured. Self-branching, very often used for planting out in summer.

'Dilly Dilly' (130) TIRET 1963 American
Calyx – pink. Corolla – double, rose-lilac. Large flowers of delicate colouring. Can be used as bush or will trail.

'Dorothea Flower' (34) THORNLEY 1969 British
Calyx – greenish white with delicate flush to underside of sweeping sepals. Corolla – single, deep lavender shaded white at the base of petals. This cv is more vigorous than its delicate appearance suggests. Does well outside during the summer as well as making a pretty greenhouse subject. Bushy, upright.

'Drame' LEMOINE 1880 French
Yet another of the *F. magellanica*-like fuchsias. Calyx scarlet with the familiar violet-

purple corolla, single, large flowers. Hardy.

'Dunrobin Bedder' MELVILLE about 1890 British

F. magellanica also played a part in the raising of this plant to judge from its flowers. These are small, red and violet. Free, hardy.

'Dr Topinard' LEMOINE 1890 French

Calyx – rose-pink, the deep rose sepals turn back. Corolla – single, white with red veins. On maturing the petals are elongated and in warm weather spread outwards. Try it in a pot on the terrace or patio.

'Dusky Rose' WALTZ 1960 American

Calyx – pink, almost coral; the green-tipped ends of the sepals bend back. Corolla – double, rose, deeper when mature. Flower is very full with ruffled petals. An eyecatcher when displayed in a basket. Cascade.

'Dutch Mill' (**70**) American

Calyx – rose-red with the long sepals held straight up. Corolla – single, blue-violet paling towards the base, a few red lines on petals. Very large, open flower on an upright, tall growing plant.

'Elizabeth' WHITEMAN 1944 British

Calyx – rose, each sepal bear-ing a green tip. Corolla – single, rose-red. Long slender flowers on this rather untidy grower which demands plenty of space.

'Empress of Prussia' (**51**) HOPPE 1868 German

Calyx — scarlet. Corolla – single, magenta. Large flowers for a hardy plant as this is, very prolific blooming. A very old cv that has been re-introduced. An unusual feature of the flowers is the large proportion that bear five sepals.

'Enfant Prodigue' (**'Pro-digy'**) LEMOINE 1887 French

It has been suggested that *F. magellanica* 'Riccartonii' was one of the parents of this useful hardy cv. With red and royal purple semi-double or double flowers it will be found to be a strong grower reaching a height of 3 ft or more in one season even if killed back almost to ground level by winter cold.

'Easter Bonnet' WALTZ 1955 American

Calyx – white with rose flush, broad sepals sweep up. Corolla – double, dusky rose-pink darkening toward the centre of the flower. Bush or basket.

'Evelyn Little' GREEN 1930 American

Calyx – pale rose then rose-red. Corolla – single, lilac-blue flecked maroon. Strong pendulous grower.

F. excorticata New Zealand (Section Skinnera)

Flowers solitary from the axils, green then purple, about $1\frac{1}{2}$ in. in length on long pedicels. These spring flowers are followed by edible purple berries which the Maoris call konini fruit. Foliage about 5 in. in length, thin, shiny green above, white below. Forms a tree in the wild to 30 ft with characteristic loose papery bark. The timber, kotukutuka wood, is attractively grained and is used in New Zealand for the manufacture of many small articles. In Britain it will make a wide, spreading shrub or small tree in the mildest parts only.

'Purpurescens' (**'Purpurea'**) A bronze foliage form listed by the leading New Zealand nurserymen.

'Falling Stars' (31) REITER 1941 American

Calyx – red. Corolla – single, dusky red. Medium size flowers in quantity. Very effective as a climber, a form that is relatively easy to produce due to the weeping or arching growth. Cascade.

'Fancy Pants' (160) REEDSTROM 1961 American

Calyx – bright red, sepals re-

curve. Corolla – double, purple-red with pink markings then rose-purple. Medium size flowers, almost round. Basket, bush or will train upright.

'Fan Dancer' FUCHSIA FOREST 1962 American

Calyx – red; sepals hang downward. Corolla – semi-double, pink and blue with red markings. Blooms are long lasting and very colourful. Trailer.

'Fascination' LEMOINE 1905 French

Calyx – bright red. Corolla – double, rose-pink. Vigorous, grows to a pyramid shape almost naturally. This plant was originally called 'Emile de Wildeman' but changed to its present name when first introduced into Britain. It has also been known as 'Pink Ballet Girl' in Britain and 'Irwin's Giant Pink' in America.

'Fiery Spider' MUNKNER 1960 American

Tube – deep carmine, long; sepals – pale salmon, thin, long. Corolla – single, crimson with hint of orange. Vigorous, continuous flowering. Cascade.

'Fiona' (58) CLARKE 1962 British

Calyx – creamy-white, very long sepals. Corolla – single, deep lilac then reddish-purple.

Flowers of good size, long lasting. Bushy if pinched out when young or will form long pendant branches.

'Flair' **(145)** TIRET 1961 American
Long white buds striped wine red. On opening, the sepals display pale magenta beneath. The semi-double corolla is rosy-mauve, flaring out when mature. Although a semi-trailer the stems are stiff so can be trained to a large bush.

'Flash' **(46)** HAZARD American
Flowers – bright red, small. Pale green foliage against which the blooms display well. Hardy, will grow to 3 ft.

'Flashlight' **(62)** GADSBY 1971 British
Small, single, pale pink flowers. Light green foliage. Hardy, dwarf, upright. This seedling of *F. magellanica molinae* is said to be better in part-shade in a hot climate.

'Flirtation Waltz' **(12)** WALTZ 1962 American
Calyx – cream with pink flush to the underside of spreading sepals. Corolla – double, clear shell pink. Red anthers contrast nicely with the pale shade of the petals. Pale green foliage. A beautiful plant and one of the most distinct of all the fuchsias. Upright, bushy.

'Florentina' TIRET 1960 American
Calyx – frosty white with sepals that curve up. Corolla – 'smokey burgundy red', wedge-shaped. Large flowers from long tapering buds. Bush or trailer.

'Flying Cloud' **(172)** REITER 1959 American
Calyx – white with pink markings. Corolla – double, white, rose tinted. Large flowers that take the heat well without flagging. Upright, basket.

'Forget-me-Not' **(33)** NEIDER-HOLZER 1940 American
Calyx – pale flesh-pink. Corolla – single, light blue. Small flowers but free. Upright. An earlier plant with the same name was introduced in Britain by Banks. This had single red and white flowers.

'Forward Look' GADSBY 1973 British
Sepals – china-rose with green tips. Corolla – single, wistaria blue then violet. Close-jointed upright bush with flowers that are held horizontally from the plant.

'Frenchi' WALTZ 1953 American
Tube – white flushed pink; sepals – salmon, thick, crepe-like, recurving. Corolla – double, silver-blue with

splashes of soft rose. Upright.

F. fulgens Mexico (Section Eufuchsia)

Shrub to 6 ft with soft woody stems tinged with red; leaves opposite, large, broadly ovate (almost heart-shaped). Flowers, dull scarlet tube, yellowish sepals, bright red corolla. The long slender flowers are in drooping clusters. An attractive greenhouse shrub in its own right but of more interest to those who grow the modern fuchsias for the part it played as an ancestor to many of them.

'Gartenmeister Bonstedt' BONSTEDT 1905 German

An *F. triphylla* type with rich orange tubular flowers against blue-green foliage. Upright. Like others of this group it needs a slightly higher winter temperature to come through unharmed.

'Gay Fandango' (**131**) NELSON 1957 American

Calyx – white with blush of pink, carmine on inside of long, broad, spreading sepals. Corolla – double, rose. Grow as a bush or try this vigorous grower on a trellis in the greenhouse.

'Georgana' TIRET 1955 American

Calyx – pink. Corolla – double, pastel blue, pink and lavender.

Large flowers in succession throughout the season. Upright, vigorous.

'Genii' REITER 1951 American

Calyx – cerise. Corolla – single, violet then reddish-purple. Small flowers. Plant forms a small upright bush, the red stems clothed with delicate lime-yellow leaves. Better when grown in full sunlight.

'Gloire de Marche' CROUSSE French

Calyx – red. Corolla – double, white veined red. Bushy. Makes a good indoor pot-plant.

'Golden Dawn' (**120**) HAAG 1951 American

Calyx – pale salmon. Corolla – single, orange-pink. Lustrous green foliage. A strong growing plant of great merit which will do well as a standard.

'Golden Marinka' (**75**) WEBER 1955 American

Upper leaf surfaces are golden variegated, with the under leaf surface wine coloured. Single flowers are red with darker red corolla. Owing to its pendulous growth it makes a perfect subject for a hanging basket.

'Graf Witte' (**40**) LEMOINE 1899 French

Calyx – carmine. Corolla – single, purple, then mauve. Small flowers on a low, rather spreading bush. Light green foliage. Hardy. Grows to 3 ft.

'Granada' (88) SCHNABEL 1957
American

Calyx – carmine-red. Corolla –
double, rich purple with a red
flash to the base of each petal.
Large flowers. Sturdy, upright
grower and as the raiser des-
cribes it, 'fool-proof'.

'Great Scott!' TIRET 1960
American

Calyx – carmine-rose. Corolla –
double, jasper red. Very large
blooms. Upright, vigorous.

'Gruss aus dem Bodethal'
(134) TEUPEL 1904 German

Calyx – bright red. Corolla –
single sometimes semi-double,
dark purple. Small flowered,
much branched plant that
'breaks' readily. The rather
lengthy name means 'Greetings
from the Bodethal'.

'Guinevere' DALE 1950 American

Calyx – white, green tipped
sepals. Corolla – semi-double,
blue-violet then purple-violet.
Long spreading sepals give an
air of elegance to this strong
grower. Spreading growth.

'Heart Throb' HODGES 1963
American

Calyx – white with carmine
blush to underside of sepals.
Corolla – double, pale blue
with white at base of petals. As
the corolla matures it spreads

wide revealing extra petals of
rose. Tall, upright grower.

'Heidi Ann' (66) SMITH 1969
British

Calyx – cerise. Corolla –
double, pale heather purple.
Nice dark green foliage. Medium size flowers in profusion,
a sturdy, bushy plant.

'Heirloom' KENNETT 1968
American

Calyx – pink, sepals deeper.
Corolla – double, lavender-
purple with heavy pink and
white marbling. Bush or trailer.

'Henriette Ernst' (119)
Netherlands

An attractive single flowered
cv with red calyx and violet-
blue corolla. Bush.

'Henri Poincaré' LEMOINE
1905 French

Calyx – bright red, sepals held
upright. Corolla – single, violet-
purple with red veins, good
size flower. Weatherproof outside during the summer months
if placed in a sunny position.
Standard.

'Hidcote Beauty' WEBB 1949
British

Calyx – creamy-white, sepals
wax-like. Corolla – single, salmon shaded rose. Bush or
basket. Cascade.

'Hindu Belle' (179) MUNKNER
1959 American

Tube – white; sepals – white,

[163]

broad, rose flush beneath. Corolla – single, rich plum purple then more red. Not free branching but flowers well.

'Howlett's Hardy' HOWLETT 1952 British
Calyx – bright red. Corolla – single, rich purple veined scarlet, bell-shaped. Hardy, vigorous grower more spreading than upright. Grows to 3 ft.

'Ice Cream Soda' CASTRO 1972 American
Tube – greenish becoming white; sepals – white or pale pink. Corolla – semi-double, inner petals white with pink markings, outer petals pink, rather ragged. Best in part shade. Bush or trailer.

'Illusion' KENNETT 1966 American
Calyx – white. Corolla – semi-double, pale blue then lavender streaked with white. Petals well flared out. Trailer or basket.

'Impudence' (26) SCHNABEL 1957 American
Calyx – red with long sepals. Corolla – single, white with red veins. The four large petals open out almost flat displaying the long, prominent red stamens. Upright or bush.

'Indian Maid' (98) WALTZ 1962 American
Calyx – bright red, extra long recurving sepals. Corolla – double, rich purple. Large shapely blooms. Imposing when grown in a basket.

'Jack Ackland' HAAG 1952 American
Calyx – bright pink. Corolla – single, deep rose then pink. Flowers of good size. Upright bush.

'Jack of Hearts' FUCHSIA FOREST 1967 American
Calyx – pink or red. Corolla – double, white with deep pink flush at base of petals, pink veins. Large flowers, trailing.

'Jack Shahan' (57) TIRET 1948 American
Flowers single, of a clear shade of pink. The growth of this universal favourite is spreading, making the plant suitable for a basket, bush or standard. Cascade.

'Jamboree' REITER 1955 American
Very large double flowers of deep carmine with irregular edges to the petals. The calyx-tube and sepals are the same colour but slightly paler. Large glossy foliage. This upright plant needs pinching regularly to make it break.

'Joan Cooper (28) WOOD 1954 British
Calyx – rose with distinct green tips to sepals. Corolla – single,

bright cherry red. This small flowered plant is said to be hardy but we find it grows better with protection. Upright in growth; needs to be 'stopped' once or twice or will make long spreading branches.

'Joan Pacey' GADSBY 1972 British

Tube – white; sepals – pink with green tips. Corolla – single, phlox pink. The red stamens show up well against the petals of the bi-coloured flower. Long flowering season and adaptable, will make a bush or standard.

'John Marsh' SCHNABEL 1953 American

Calyx – white. Corolla – double, pale orchid pink. This sport from 'Shalimar' has a pale blue, tightly packed corolla. A very pretty pastel shade bloom. This plant and the parent have similar trailing growth. Basket.

'Joy Patmore' (**64**) TURNER 1961 British

Calyx – white, short tube and sepals. Corolla – single, carmine-purple with white patch at the base of each petal. Flower of delightful colour contrast. Upright. Bush or standard.

'Juno' KENNETT 1966 American

Calyx – white. Corolla – single or semi-double, deep red then clear red. A striking flower with narrow reflexed sepals and long brightly coloured petals. Trailing. Fine in a large pot or basket.

'Kernan Robson' TIRET 1958 American

Calyx – pale red, sepals reflex right back against the tube. Corolla – double, 'smokey-red' then rose-red, large flowers. Upright, bushy. Standard.

'Keystone' (**111**) HAAG 1945 American

Calyx – pale carmine-rose. Corolla – single, pale pink. The tube has deep pink stripes which adds considerably to the effect of the flower. Very free. Pleasing foliage. Upright.

'King's Ransom' (**68**) SCHNABEL 1954 American

Tube – white then palest red; sepals – white with green tips, pale pink beneath. Corolla – double, purple-blue then clear purple; the base of each petal is marked with pale pink. Vigorous, upright.

'Kolding Perle' (**127**) ? Danish

An attractive flower with long tube to the cream calyx and single cerise corolla (the flower is somewhat similar to the very old 'Amy Lye'). As the Kolding

[165]

Botanic Garden is in Denmark it seems probable that this was the original home of the free flowering plant. Upright.

'Kon Tiki' (82) TIRET 1965 American
Calyx – white, distinct green tips to the sepals. Corolla – double, deep purple-blue. Not the easiest of plants to grow to perfection but such a valuable addition to the range of colours that the cool conditions required are worth providing. Bush, trailer.

'Kwintet' (65) VAN WIERINGEN 1970 Netherlands
Deep rose single flowers with the corolla a slightly deeper shade. Easy grower flowering continuously throughout the summer. A good bedder.

'La Campanella' BLACKWELL 1968 British
Tube – pale pink; sepals – white with pink flush. Corolla – semi-double, violet then purple. The base of each petal is white. Reliable cv with small profuse flowers to form a short standard or ideally to grow in a basket. 'La Campanella' (the little bell) by Paganini, originally a Caprice for violin, is a fitting name for this delightful plant with its masses of little bells.

'Lady Isobel Barnett' (63) GADSBY 1971 British

Calyx – rose-red with neatly recurved sepals. Corolla – single, pale rose with deep rose veins. Free flowering, the blooms facing outwards rather than down. Good for bedding out, greenhouse or showing. Compact, upright.

'Lady Thumb' ROE 1967 British
This sport from 'Tom Thumb' has red and white single flowers. Hardy, profuse, grows to only 1 ft.

'La Fiesta' (22) KENNETT 1962 American
Calyx – creamy-white, green tips to sepals. Corolla – double, centre petals dianthus purple; outer petals although similar in colour have many white markings and on maturing these petals stand out to produce a bloom of exquisite form and grace. Semi-trailing.

'Lakeside' THORNLEY 1968 British
Calyx – deep pink, green tipped sepals. Corolla – single or semi-double, light blue, pink veined. Changes to lilac on maturing. A free growing floriferous trailer.

'La Neige' (187) TIRET 1965 American
Calyx – white with feint blush, sepals soft pink beneath. Corolla – double, cream. Rounded

flowers, a beautiful bloom, good robust grower too. Growth is more spreading than upright.

'Laura' (**196**) MARTIN 1968 American
Calyx – bright red. Corolla – double, sky-blue then lavender. Large flowers with waved petals. Bush or trailer. A single flowered cv with the same name introduced in America in 1946 does not appear to be in cultivation in Britain.

'Lena' (**77**) BUNNEY 1862 British
Calyx – creamy white then pale flesh, green tips to sepals. Corolla – semi-double or double, magenta then rose-magenta. Hardy in a sheltered spot. An outstanding plant grown inside or out although of different appearance when treated as a tender subject. Nice in a basket, it will also grow to a standard.

'Lena Dalton' (**3**) REIMERS 1953 American
Calyx – cream with pale blush, deeper colour under the four cup-shaped sepals. Corolla – double, deep slate-blue then mauve-pink with bright red anthers. Neat bush shape. Many dainty flowers which

although small are of perfect form.

'Leonora' (**115**) TIRET 1960 American
Calyx – pink with deep pink stripes to tube. Corolla – single, clear pink, bell-shaped. A free flowering plant with blooms of classic shape in a clear yet strong colour.

'Leverkusen' (**'Leverhulme'**) HARTNAUER 1928 German
Clusters of long-tubed cerise flowers. Pleasing green foliage. A random seedling from 'Andenken an Heinrich Henkel' this is one of those plants that needed a name change in order to sell them in Britain even years after World War 1.

'Liebriez' (**104**) KOHENE 1874 German
Calyx – cerise. Corolla – semi-double, pale cerise heavily veined in red. Abundant flowers, smallish of an attractive shade. A re-discovery of recent years, this plant is now frequently to be seen as a 'show' specimen. Bushy, compact, fairly hardy.

'Lilac Lustre' (**84**) MUNKNER 1961 American
Calyx – deep rose-red, broad upturned sepals. Corolla – double, powder-blue. Large well-filled blooms. This up-

right grower has shining deep green foliage.

'Lolita' TIRET 1963 American
Calyx – white with rose markings. Corolla – double, clear blue then lilac. A beautiful flower in which the shining rose underpart of the sepals is well displayed as the sepals roll back. Growth is of the cascade type.

'Lollypop' (20) WALKER-JONES 1950 American
Calyx – cream; sepals – soft pink, thick, sweeping up. Corolla – single, deep plum. Very long petals. Natural growth is trailing but can be trained to a variety of forms.

'Lonely Ballerina' BLACK-well 1962 British
Calyx – deep carmine, broad sweeping sepals. Corolla – double, white with red veins and markings. Large flowers. Trailing. This is a good selling name, not that this plant needs it, for people are often reminded of a ballerina when looking at the flowers of a double fuchsia.

'Lord Lonsdale' (122) HOW-LETT 1943 British
Calyx – cream with green tips to the sepals. Corolla – single, tangerine-pink. Large light green foliage which often curls inwards.

'Lord Roberts' (133) LE-MOINE 1909 French
Calyx – scarlet, very thick shiny sepals. Corolla – single, purple-violet with red veins and rose flush to base of petals. Large flowers, upright.

'Louise Emershaw' (110) TIRET 1972 American
Calyx – white with long sepals having a magenta flush to the underneath. Corolla – double, jasper-red. A natural trailer. Basket.

'Lovable' (69) ERICKSON 1963 American
Calyx – red. Corolla – double, clear pink. An immaculate flower. Strong grower although the stems will need support for the heavy blooms. Good greenhouse plant. Can be trained as an open bush.

'Lucky Strike' (147) NEIDER-HOLZER 1943 American
Calyx – cream, rose undersides to sepals. Corolla – semi-double, blue with clear rose markings, outer petals waved, pink with purple shadows. Upright or bush but can be used in a basket or planter by pinching well.

'Lye's Unique' (55) LYE 1886 British
Calyx – waxy-white, long, rather fat tube; spreading sepals, short. Corolla – single,

salmon-orange. Upright, quick grower, will make a standard of perfect symmetry.

'Lyric' (148) KENNETT 1964 American

Calyx – white, pink flush. Corolla – double, rose and various shades of pink. Petals long, forming a narrow corolla. The name is said to stem from the fact that the petaloids resemble the notes on a musical scale.

'Madame Cornelissen' CORNELISSEN 1860

Calyx – crimson. Corolla – single or semi-double, white veined with cerise. Hardy, upright to 1 m (3 ft). Easy to train as a standard. An old favourite still widely planted today.

'Madame Van der Strass' (14)

Red and white double medium size flowers. Very free. Bush or pyramid.

F. magellanica Southern Chile, Argentina (Section Quelusia)

Dainty flowers with prominent stamens carried in showy profusion for many months. Hardy over all of Britain, the degree of damage to living wood depending on locality. In the parts of the country where little damage occurs, large specimens of some cvs or varieties may be seen. These are sometimes as high as 3–4 m (9–12 ft) but in less clement areas they are often reduced to ground level in winter, with growth shooting out again in the spring to repeat the display the following summer and autumn. The species is variable in the wild with at least three *vars*. Some introductions from South America where all three are found are possibly hybrids between two of these three sub-species from the same area. Although sometimes listed as *vars*. for the sake of simplicity (and we hope accuracy) we treat them here as cvs. Two of the natural sub-species or *vars* are also in cultivation on a general scale and these are numbered with the best of the hardy fuchsias.

F.m. alba see **F.m.var. molinae**

F.m. 'Conica'. A robust growing wild 'find'. See also note under 'Riccartonii'.

F.m. 'Corallina'. Scarlet and purple single flowers. Vigorous with spreading branches.

F.m. 'Discolor'. Dwarf, very hardy. The typical red and purple flowers.

F.m. 'Globosa'. Buds almost round, flowers short. Colour as the foregoing.

F.m. var. macrostema ('Gracilis'). (47). Tall, reaching 2 m (6 ft). Stems arch gracefully when festooned with masses of slender flowers. This and 'Riccartonii' are the plants to be seen in cottage gardens along the western seaboard of the British Isles. Naturalised in South-west England, Ireland and the Orkneys.

F.m. var. molinae (F. magellanica alba). Tiny flowers, white then pale flesh pink. Foliage pale green. Upright, bushy, very hardy. Seldom completely cut back by cold weather. For maximum flowers plant in a hot sunny spot in poor soil.

F.m. 'Pumila'. A gem for the rockery or border. Bushy, very compact, it bears the typical flowers but on a reduced scale. Plant in small groups for the best effect.

F.m. 'Riccartonii'. This, one of the most popular of hardy fuchsias (and rightly so) originated at Riccarton, near Edinburgh about 1830. A single chance seedling with *F. magellanica* 'Conica' usually cited as one of the parents. It is a robust grower, very free with its flowers. These differ from the other tall members of this group in that the flowers have more blue in the colouring of the corolla and the sepals are generally more broad. One of the finest of all to form a hedge where a height of up to 1.5 m (nearly 5 ft) can be expected.

F.m. 'Variegata' Green foliage edged in cream or yellow with pink flush against which the elegant red and purple flowers are well displayed.

F.m. 'Versicolor' or **'Tricolor' (44).** Grey leaves heavily stained red or pink become variegated green and cream on maturing. Slender red and purple blooms. Striking whether flowering or not.

'Major Heaphy' (52) British Calyx – creamy-pink, then red. Corolla – single, dusky-red. Flowers are small but plentiful. Large attractive foliage.

'Mandarin' (5) SCHNABEL 1963 American Calyx – pale pink with deeper stripes, sepals sweep up, pea-green tips. Corolla – semi-double, glowing orange-carmine. Profuse flowering. The deep green leathery foliage is an aid to the identification of this desirable plant. Trailer.

'Mantilla' REITER 1948 American Single rich carmine flowers in clusters of *F. triphylla* form. Bronze foliage. At its best in a basket or placed high up to view the very long blooms from below. Does well in sun.

'Margaret' WOOD 1937 British
Calyx – rose. Corolla – double, mauve. Good size flowers for a hardy plant that grows to 1 m (3 ft).

'Margaret Brown' WOOD 1949 British
Calyx — rose-salmon. Corolla – single, magenta. Small flowers in quantity on an erect yet compact bush. Hardy. This plant, as well as the preceding one, was named after Mrs Margaret Slater, past president of the British Fuchsia Society, by the late W. P. Wood, a friend of the Brown family.

'Margery Blake' (73) WOOD 1950 British
Calyx – scarlet. Corolla – single, purple. Small flowers in quantity from early to late on this short, rather spreading, hardy cultivar. Fine for covering spaces in the shrub border.

'Marin Glow' (91) REED-STROM 1954 American
Calyx – pure waxy-white. Corolla – single, dark purple, then magenta. An excellent cv with flowers not only of perfect form but of clean-cut appearance. Upright, will bed

out well.

'Marinka' (128) ROZAIN-BOU-CHARLAT 1902 French
Deep red single flowers with slightly darker corolla. Very free flowering, medium size blooms. Trailing growth of the type that makes it 'natural' for a basket.

'Mary' (176) BONSTEDT 1905 German
Brilliant scarlet long-tubed flowers of *F. triphylla* type. Narrow dark green foliage. Upright bush.

'Mieke Meursing' (136) HOP-GOOD 1969 British
Calyx – red, sepals curve upwards. Corolla – single, pale pink with distinct red veins, red stamens. Free branching easy grower. Popular as an exhibition pot plant, partly for its ability to produce flowers opening at the same time all over the bush. Will bed out well too.

'Melody' (1, 108) REITER 1942 American
Calyx – rose or ivory with deep pink stripes on the tube, sepals flushed beneath, curving up. Corolla – single, pale cyclamen purple with white shading at base of petals. The long pointed buds keep on and on coming. Easy growing, this cv is probably best seen as the basic

bush shape.

'Merry Mary' FUCHSIA FOREST 1965 American

Calyx – pink fading to white at ends of sepals, these are deep pink beneath. Corolla – double, white with pink stripes. Strong growth with impressive flowers for greenhouse or warm garden.

F. microphylla var. microphylla

see note under *F.* x *bacillaris*

'Midnight Sun' (158) WALTZ 1960 American

Calyx – pink with vinous-pink colouring to under sepals. Corolla – double, inner petals rich purple, outer petals magenta with splashes of pink. There is also pink at the base of petals which shows when the flower matures. Strong growing greenhouse plant that flowers well until late in the season. Upright.

'Minnesota' (113) GARSON 1938 American

Calyx – ivory-pink with large, wide, cup-shaped sepals. Corolla – single, sometimes semi-double, purple. Large flowers of similar colour to the old 'Rose of Castile' but with considerably larger blooms. Upright, good standard.

'Miss California' (100) HODGES 1950 American

Calyx – white becoming pale pink with deep pink stripes, short tube, very long pointed sepals. Corolla – single or semi-double, white with wash of pink on maturing, pink veins. A vigorous, upright grower with thin stems which make the plant useful for training to almost any form. At no time is it better than when seen as a standard (tree).

'Mission Bells' WALKER 1948 American

Calyx – bright, deep red. Corolla – single, rich purple, flared, bell-shaped. Upright, bushy, but could be used in basket.

'Molesworth' LEMOINE 1903 French

Calyx – bright red, sepals turn back. Corolla – double, white, red veins, long centre petals. Not the neatest of growers but an attractive flower. Try it in a basket.

'Monsoon' LOCKERBIE Australian

Calyx – rose-pink with green tips to sepals. Corolla – double, deep sky-blue, petals short, twisted and curled. Upright.

'Moonlight Sonata' BLACKWELL 1963 British

Calyx – bright pink, sepals recurved. Corolla – single, light purple with blush of pink at base of petals. Vigorous, upright although somewhat spreading. Adaptable, can be used as bush, standard or basket.

'Morning Light' (78) WALTZ 1960 American
Calyx – ivory with pink flush to the broad sepals that turn up at the tips; the short tube is red and this colour is carried down the edges of the sepals. Corolla – double, lavender-blue then rose-lavender with pink splashes on the outer, overlapping petals. Foliage light green, almost pale gold when grown in sunlight. Upright, spreading. A superb plant.

'Moth Blue' TIRET 1949 American
Calyx – red, short tube, long sepals. Corolla – double, deep lilac-blue. Free flowering, upright.

'Mr A. Huggett' (35) pre 1930 British
An upright growing plant of great charm. The single flowers are carried in quantity and although small are of perfect form. The calyx is light cerise and the corolla soft mauve-pink with the edges of the overlapping petals outlined in violet. Bright red anthers complete the flower. A fine subject for a cool window indoors.

'Mr W. Rundle' RUNDLE 1896 British
Calyx – cream with rose flush. Corolla – single, carmine then red. Most unusual colouring and form, a plant that we would not wish to be without. Fairly hardy, to about 1 m (3 ft).

'Mrs Churchill' (143) GARSON early 1940s American
Calyx – deep cerise, sepals wide, reflexed. Corolla – single, white but so heavily veined in cerise as to appear pink. Bushy.

'Mrs Lovell Swisher' (17) EVANS-REEVES 1942 American
Calyx – pink or ivory with flush, pink on underside of sepals, very long tube. Corolla – single, carmine to rose-red. Small flowers of dainty appearance on an upright bush.

'Mrs Popple' ELLIOT 1899 British
Calyx – deep scarlet. Corolla – violet. Hardy. Vigorous, to 1 m (3 ft).

'Mrs Rundle' RUNDLE 1883 British
Calyx – cream-pink, wax-like sepals have green tips. Corolla – single, orange-red. Will grow outside during warm weather although flowers will be longer when treated as a cool-house plant.

'Muriel' (194) pre 1930 prob-

ably British
Calyx – scarlet, sepals held upright, these also twist slightly. Corolla – single, pale blue then magenta. Large flowers on rather weak branches that can be trained easily, on a trellis, bush, climber, etc. Cascade.

'Nancy Lou' STUBBS 1971 American
Calyx – white or soft pink (depending on the amount of sun the plant is exposed to); sepals have pink flush inside and out. Corolla – double, brilliant white. Upright but compact in form.

'New Fascination' NEIDER-HOLZER 1940 American
Calyx – carmine, red underside to sepals apparent as they sweep up. Corolla – double, rose-veined cerise with red markings here and there. The petals open out almost flat in hot weather. Upright, will make a good standard. There is another plant of the same name sent out by a leading British nursery firm. So many must have been sold over the years that numbers of people who grow the second plant will not recognise this description. The incorrectly named plant which bears numerous single flowers is so pretty that we have included a picture of

it in plate 163.

'Nicola Jane' DAWSON 1959 British
Calyx – scarlet, green tips to reflexed sepals. Corolla – double, blush-pink with cerise veins to petals. Hardy, upright and bushy.

'Nina Wills' WILLS 1961 British
Calyx – pale flesh-pink. Corolla – single, baby-pink. Small flowers, very free. This weatherproof plant is eminently suitable for bedding out in summer and will make a good standard too. It was a sport from 'Forget-Me-Not'.

'Novato' SOO YUN 1972 American
Calyx – white, under sepals rose. Corolla – single, scarlet tnen salmon. Compact growing. Bush, trailer or basket is suggested.

'Omeomy' KENNETT 1963 American
Calyx – pale pink with long sepals. Corolla – double, purple overlaid with pink marbling. Robust trailer with attractive green foliage.

'Orange Drops' MARTIN 1964 American.
Calyx – pale orange. Corolla – single, deep orange. Flowers in clusters. Upright, bush. Best in sun.

'Orange Flare' (**135**) HAND-

LEY 1972 British
Calyx – orange-salmon, thick, recurved sepals. Corolla – single, petals are light orange base becoming much deeper toward the edges. Upright, strong grower. This has quite the best colour in the orange shades that we have seen. Said to be best when exposed to full sunlight.

'Orangy' REEDSTROM 1962 American
Calyx – pink with orange glow. Corolla – single, pale orange. Foliage yellowish. Vigorous trailer.

'Otherfellow' (153) HAZARD 1946 American
Calyx – white, wax-like. Corolla – single, pale apricot-rose, small flowers, very free. Upright and bushy.

'Papa Bluess' TIRET 1956 American
Tube – white; sepals – ivory to pale rose, deeper on the inside, sweeping up. Corolla – double, deep violet with rose markings at the base of petals; the corolla becomes rose-purple on maturing. Imposing flowers. Upright if staked, suited to basket training if pinched out early.

'Pathétique' (81) BLACKWELL British
Calyx – dark red. Corolla –
double, white with red veins, bright red stamens contrast nicely to enhance the purity in the white of the extra large blooms. Raised from a sport on 'Pink Ballet Girl'. Upright, bush.

'Pat Meara' (9) MILLER 1962 British
Calyx – bright cerise, sepals held straight up. Corolla – single, slate-blue then lavender, red veins. Filaments and style are also red and show up well against the petals. Upright and bushy, this will do well as a pot specimen on a sheltered patio or terrace.

'Peachy Keen' TIRET 1967 American
Calyx – rose-red. Corolla – double, salmon orange. Rather small foliage. Trailer.

'Peggy King' WOOD 1954 British
Cerise single flowers with the wide corolla deeper than the sepals. Upright and bushy, a good hardy fuchsia.

'Pee Wee Rose' ('Peewee Rose') (29) NEIDERHOLZER 1939 American
Calyx – rose. Corolla – deep pink, single. Tiny flowers in clusters borne on long, willowy branches. Small foliage. It is on record that this plant is a hybrid with *F. magellanica*

molinae as one of the parents. Basket.

'Pepi' (112) TIRET 1963 American

Calyx – white, flushed deep rose, broad incurving sepals. Corolla – double, orange-red becoming paler almost light bronze. Upright, bush or first rate standard, vigorous.

'Peppermint Stick' (150) WALKER-JONES 1950 American

Calyx – deep carmine-rose; sepals turn up. Corolla – double, inner petals violet then purple, outer petals pink with purple markings (like the writing in a peppermint stick). The corolla takes some time to fill out once the calyx has split, once it does the bloom is most striking. Upright, bush.

'Personality' (149) FUCHSIA-LA 1967 American

Calyx – bright rose-red, thick sepals extending from the short tube. Corolla – double, red with purple markings. Large flowers. Upright, bush.

'Phénoménal' (27) LEMOINE 1869 French

Calyx – bright red. Corolla – double, rich purple-violet, very full corolla with longer petals in the centre making it wedge-shaped. The large blooms need warmth to do well for in dull conditions the buds fail to open. Bush.

'Phyllis' (49) BROWN 1938 British

Calyx – rose, thick wax-like tube and sepals. Corolla – semi-double or single, rose-cerise. Profuse flowers. Hardy to 1 m (3 ft). Will make a stout standard if grown inside.

'Pink Balloon' NEIDERHOLZER 1940 American

Calyx – dark red. Corolla – single, white veined pink. Very large, loosely shaped, rather globular flowers. Upright, bush.

'Pink Bon Accorde' (106) THORNE 1959 British

Calyx – pale pink. Corolla – single, cherry. Very free. Buds face upwards but bend down to a horizontal position after opening. It is advisable to remove some of the foliage from the centre of the plant for unless a circulation of air is maintained *botrytis* can set in at this point. Bush, tall.

'Pink Chiffon' WALTZ 1966 American

Calyx – white with pink flush. Corolla – double, soft pink deepening at the base of petals. Blooms are globular in shape. A trailer suitable for basket.

'Pink Cloud' WALTZ 1956 American

Tube – white; sepals – pink, long, wide, sweep up and twist at tips. Corolla – single, clear pink. Large flower with four broad, overlapping petals. Adaptable for training as bush, pillar or espalier.

'Pink Darling' (38) MACHADO 1966 American
Tube – deep pink; sepals – pale pink with distinct green tips. Corolla – single, pale magenta. Small flowers, facing outwards from the plant. Good bedding plant.

'Pink Fairy' (144) WALTZ 1954 American
Calyx – soft pink, sepals broad, held up. Corolla double, off white to pale pink depending on the siting of the plant. The mature blooms open wide. Thick green leaves provide a perfect foil. Bush.

'Pink Flamingo' FUCHSIA FOREST – CASTRO 1961 American
Calyx – deep pink, long, narrow, curling sepals. Corolla – semi-double, pale pink, dark pink veins extend from the base of petals. Bronze-green foliage. Upright, slender bush. Aptly named, for the flower colour is remarkably like that of the flamingo.

'Pink Galore' (60) FUCHSIA-LA 1961 American
Delightful candy-pink double flowers. The upturned sepals are slightly deeper in colour than the corolla. Dark green glossy foliage. The natural habit is trailing so will make a good basket plant. Cascade.

'Pink Marshmallow' STUBBS 1971 American
Tube – white, short; sepals – white with pink flush underneath, arching. Corolla – double, white with pink shading, deep pink veins. Very large flower. Growth is vigorous, trailing.

'Pink Pearl' (50) BRIGHT 1919 British
A semi-double rose flowered cv of merit. The medium size blooms are carried right through the season, inside or out. Upright. Bush.

'Pink Quartette' WALKER-JONES 1949 American
Calyx – pink, deep pink or red depending on position, sepals turn back. Corolla – semi-double, pink. The outer petals roll into four tubes on the mature flower – hence the name. Upright.

'Pink Temptation' WILLS 1969 British
A sport from 'Temptation' with a similar habit of growth. The flowers in this case are pale cream sepals and tube with the

single corolla a pleasing shade of rose.

'Pinwheel' WALTZ 1958 American

Calyx – pale red, short tube, broad sepals turned back. Corolla – semi-double, soft violet. The flower opens out flat to resemble a pinwheel in form. A novel yet beautiful bloom. Upright, self-branching, bush.

'Pixie' RUSSELL 1960 British

Calyx – red. Corolla – single, violet-blue then mauve. This useful colour in hardy fuchsias was found by Richard Draper, the glasshouse foreman of Russell's Windlesham nursery growing as a sport on 'Graf Witte'. It too, has the same light green foliage of the parent to add to its other fine points. Hardy to 1 m (3 ft).

'Port Arthur' (**188**) STORY 1869 British

Calyx – red, cup-shaped sepals. Corolla – double, violet-purple then magenta. Flowers small to medium on well branched, upright bush. The fresh green leaves are an added attraction to this desirable plant.

'Prelude' (**162**) KENNETT 1958 American

Calyx – double, white with pink showing from beneath the sepals as the flower opens. Corolla – double, purple centre petals; outer petals are mainly white but also have pink and purple markings. Trailer, but not of the type to be put in a basket and more suited to be a well supported bush. This is also sold as 'American Prelude' in Britain to distinguish it from an earlier cv with the name 'Prelude'. In New Zealand it is listed as 'Prelude of America'.

'Prince of Orange' BANKS 1872 British

Calyx – pale rose with tangerine glow. Corolla – single, deep orange. Wax-like flowers in heavy clusters. Upright.

'Princess Dollar' (**105**) LE-MOINE 1912 French

Calyx – cerise-red. Corolla – double, rich purple becoming magenta-purple. Smallish flowers, free. Bush, self-branching.

F. procumbens New Zealand (Section Skinnera)

A tiny grower with small yellow flowers in which the purple sepals are completely reflexed. There is no corolla. The small blooms are followed by comparatively large fruits that resemble small red plums. Foliage is almost round and is produced from tiny stems that hug the ground. Hardy. Suitable for a hanging basket, as a rock plant and as ground cover in its country of origin.

'Purple Heart' WALKER-JONES 1950 American

Calyx – crimson, long tube and sepals, wax-like. Corolla – double, violet, outer petals pink. Large blooms on willowy branches. Trailer.

'Quasar' WALKER-FUCHSIA-LA American

Calyx – white with green tips to sepals, turning back. Corolla – double, blue with white markings to outer petals, then light purple and pale pink. Very large blooms which appear to be blue and white until inspected more closely. Trailer.

'Queen Mary' (118) HOWLETT 1911 British

Calyx – pale pink with white tips to sepals. Corolla – single, rose-pink then mauve. Strong grower that needs the restriction of a large pot to induce plentiful flowers.

R.A.F.' ('Royal Air Force') **146)** GARSON 1942 American

Calyx – light red. Corolla – double, rose with red veins, nicely waved petals. Small dark foliage with red marking to the leaf-margins. Bush.

Rambling Rose' TIRET 1959 American

Clear rose double flowers, an unusual shade in trailing fuch-

sias. Perfect in a basket.

'Raspberry' (103) TIRET 1959 American

Calyx – pink with some white toward the tips of the sepals. Corolla – double, clear raspberry-rose (pink with a hint of blue) becoming rose on maturing. Very large flowers, although not very freely produced. It has such unusual colouring that a place on the greenhouse staging is assured. Upright or bush.

'Red Ribbons' (71) MARTIN 1959 American

Calyx – clear red, very long, twisting sepals. Corolla – double, white. Similar to 'Texas Longhorn' in general appearance. This one will do well outside when planted out as summer bedding. Useful inside too where the upright stems can be trained to an open bush.

'Red Shadows' WALTZ 1962 American

Calyx – crimson, sepals upturned. Corolla – double, deep purple then ruby. The petals are attractively ruffled. Bush, rather low, so will also be suitable for basket.

'Red Spider' (30) REITER 1946 American

Calyx – deep crimson, extra long, narrow, pendant sepals.

Corolla – single, rose-madder edged with crimson. Small foliage, large flowers for such a slender plant. Best in a basket. Cascade.

'Red Wing' TIRET 1949 American

Calyx – red, long sepals. Corolla – single, plum purple. Trailer.

'Regal Robe' (83) ERICKSON-LEWIS 1959 American

Calyx – deep red. Corolla – double, deep violet then royal purple, deep pink marking at the base of the petals. Some of the petals are uneven giving highlights to accentuate the richness of colour. Upright, tall but more spreading when in flower.

F. regia var. alpestris Brazil (Section Quelusia)

A semi-climbing or rambling shrub which can reach a height of 6 m (19 ft) in the wild and almost that under protected cultivation. The single flowers carried singly in the upper leaf axils have red sepals and purple corolla. Large leathery leaves downy on both leaf-surfaces, downy young shoots. Said to be fairly hardy in the very mildest parts of Britain but this we query.

'Rhapsody' (171) BLACKWELL 1965 British

Calyx – deep blood red. Corolla – semi-double, white with red veins. Spreading petals display red stamens. Strong upright, bush.

'Rigoletto' (10) BLACKWELL British

Calyx – deep red. Corolla – double, violet then light purple. The almost triangular buds open to reveal a corolla in which the petals have frilled edges, pretty flower. Upright, bush.

'Rosecroft Beauty' EDEN 1969 British

A foliage plant of merit with red and yellow leaf-margins. A sport on 'Snowcap', this has similar colour flowers and the same habit of growth.

'Rose of Castile' (114) BANKS 1869 British

Calyx – white with rose flush to green-tipped sepals. Corolla – single, purple with white base to each petal. Hardy. A fine dwarf plant to grow in the garden or inside as a pot plant.

'Rose of Castile (Improved)' (21) LANE 1871 British

Calyx – pale pink, sepals flesh with green tips. Corolla – single, violet then reddish purple. More vigorous and larger in all its parts than the foregoing, it is recommended for training as a standard.

Only as a bush is it hardy.
'Royal Purple' (53) ? LEMOINE
1896 French
Bright shining red and purple
single flowers (sometimes
throws a semi-double). An
imposing plant if the true cv
can be found.

The query about the raiser
is due to the fact that this plant
is sometimes said to be of
British origin. Upright, robust.
'Royal Touch' (4) TIRET 1964
American
Calyx – cream, rose underside
to sepals. Corolla – double,
royal purple then magenta.
Trailer.
'Royal Velvet' WALTZ 1962
American
Calyx – crimson. Corolla –
double, deep velvet purple
with crimson shades to impart a
sheen to the waved petals.
Very full flower on a neat
growing plant. Bush.
'Ruffled Petticoats' FOSTER
1974 American
Calyx – deep pink, sepals short.
Corolla – double, white with a
hint of rose. Beautifully ruffled
petals. Trailer.
'Ruffles' (173) ERICKSON 1960
American
Calyx – deep pink, short tube,
broad upturned sepals. Corolla
– double, deep violet with pink
inner petals, ruffled – of course!

Most attractive, free flowering.
Fine basket plant.
'Rufus' ('The Red') (93)
NELSON 1951 American
Flowers clear red (usually des-
cribed as turkey red) single, of
moderate size. Plant is vigor-
ous, upright and in every way
reliable. Standard.
'Sally Ann' PENNISI 1971
American
Calyx – white with pink flush,
sepals soft pink beneath, green
tips. Corolla – double, various
shades of pink and lavender.
An attractive flower in which
the sepals are held straight out.
Basket.

F. sanctae-rosae Bolivia,
Peru (Section Eufuchsia)
Shrub of variable form growing
from 0.5 m to 3 m (1 ft 6 in. to
10 ft) in height. Flowers spring
from the upper leaf axils, tube
long with sepals extending past
the corolla. Tube – red; sepals
– scarlet. Corolla – single,
scarlet. A desirable shrub for a
greenhouse collection.
'San Diego' (87) TIRET 1964
American
Calyx – pinkish-white. Corolla
– double, rose-red. Huge
blooms. Trailer, bush.
'Sarong' (156) KENNETT 1963
American
Calyx – white with pink flush,

deeper on the underside of the long, twisting sepals. Corolla – double, violet then magenta with noticeable pink splodges. A long bloom of interesting form. Upright but rather floppy.

'Satellite' KENNETT 1965 American

Calyx – white, spreading sepals shaded magenta beneath. Corolla – single, dark red with bold streaks of white on both sides of petals; on maturing the corolla lightens to bright red. The four large petals give the bloom a striking appearance. Upright making a tall bush.

'Sea Shell' ('Seashells') EVANS 1954 American

Calyx – white to phlox-pink. Corolla – double, clear pink with outer petals presenting a shell-like effect. Novel but very pretty too. Bush.

'Sensation' MUNKNER 1962 American

Calyx – shining pink, deepest on the very long narrow sepals. Corolla – single, deep violet, waved edges. Trailer. Basket.

'Shady Blue' (**165**) GADSBY 1971 British

Calyx – carmine-pink, wide, spreading sepals. Corolla – single, violet-blue shaded with pink at base of petals. Flowers large, of good substance. Very

free flowering. Upright, branching. Bush.

'Shady Lane' WALTZ 1959 American

Calyx – coral-pink with green tips to the broad recurved sepals. Corolla – double, lilac marbled with coral, very full corolla with overlapping petals. Strong willowy branches. Trailer. Basket.

'Shangri-La' MARTIN 1963 American

Calyx – dark pink or red. Corolla – double, pale pink or almost white with red veins then clear pink. Large, heavy flower. Bush.

'Shasta' KENNETT 1964 American

Calyx – pale pink. Corolla – semi-double or double, white with pink markings to the outer petals Petals have distinct serrated edges. Trailer. Bush.

'Shooting Star' (**157**) MARTIN 1965 American

Calyx – salmon red, long sepals. Corolla – double, deep purple with salmon streaks on the outer petals. A beautiful flower of unusual form resembling a comet more than a shooting star. Trailer will bush.

'Shy Look' GADSBY 1972 British

Several flowers spring from each leaf node on this interesting plant. They are single, crimson and light purple but instead of hanging downwards as do most fuchsias they face out away from the centre of the plant. An upright bush in form, it was a seedling from 'Upward Look'.

'Sierra Blue' (24) WALTZ 1957 American
Calyx – white, short tube, sepals flushed pink beneath. Corolla – double, silvery-blue then soft lilac. Upright, rather arching growth.

F. simplicicaulis Peru (Section Eufuchsia)
Shrub to 4.5 m (over 14 ft) when growing through other plants in the wild and reaching a similar height if allowed to grow unchecked in the greenhouse. Slender long-tubed flowers of 5 cm (2 in.) bright red, in drooping clusters. Large leaves in groups of four carried on short petioles.

'Sleigh Bells' (89) SCHNABEL 1954 American
Pure white single flowers of perfect form. The long rather narrow sepals curl around completely to display the rounded bell-like corolla. Best flowers are to be seen on plants growing in a shady, well ventilated glasshouse. Give them sun and the sepals turn pink.

Growth is upright, rather stiff.

'So Big' WALTZ 1955 American
Calyx – pink, narrow tube is deep pink. Corolla – double, white, very large bloom. A leafy, robust grower. Trailer.

'Snowcap' (166) HENDERSON British
Calyx – bright red. Corolla – semi-double or double, clear white with a few red veins that radiate from the base of the petals, medium size flowers produced in quantity. Easy, entirely reliable. Bush, pyramid or standard.

'Sonata' (90) TIRET 1960 American
Calyx – pale pink with deep pink lines extending down the tube and along the sepals. Corolla – double, white, very large, full. Semi-trailer but makes a large upright bush with training.

'Sophisticated Lady' (155) MARTIN 1964 American
Calyx – soft pink. The long pointed sepals extend well over the very full corolla. Corolla – double, white. Something special for a basket.

'Southgate' WALKER-JONES 1951 American
Tube – greenish white; sepals – pale pink, deeper on reverse. Corolla – double, pale pink with deep pink veins. One of

the largest blooms of the pink doubles. Strong growing, it will make a good standard.

'Speciosa' ('Fulgens Speciosa') Garden origin

Several plants have been sent out under this name in the past. The one usually supplied is probably a seedling from *F. fulgens*. It is very free flowering with a rather shorter tube than the presumed parent. For the greenhouse border.

F. splendens Mexico (Section Eufuchsia)

Shrub to small tree with hairy twigs and almost heart-shaped leaves; these are carried on long stalks. Tube – red, long; sepals – scarlet with green tips. Corolla – single, yellow-green. Flowers are produced from the axils of the reduced leaves. A beautiful greenhouse subject.

'Spotlight' (199) SMITH 1970 British

Calyx – deep pink. Corolla – single or semi-double, white with sparse red veins. A splendid trailing plant raised by nurseryman John Smith. Basket.

'Spring Bells' (191) KOOIJMAN 1972 Netherlands

Calyx – bright red. Corolla – semi-double, clear white. Immaculate flowers carried over the whole season plus neat

shape of the plant are the points to mark this recent introduction for a good future. Bush.

'Strawberry Delight' (23) GADSBY 1970 British

Calyx – crimson, glossy. Corolla – double, white with red veins, flushed pale strawberry on outer petals. Small flowers, very free. Foliage golden green with bronze veins. Thin wiry stems, much branched growth. Bush, basket.

'Strawberry Sundae' (96) KENNETT 1958 American

Calyx – ivory, tube short, sepals broad. Corolla – double, pale lilac then pink. Very large blooms. Trailer. Would need a large basket.

'Summer Snow' WALTZ 1956 American

Calyx – pure white, tube short, sepals recurve. Corolla – semi-double, cream at first then pure white. Medium size flowers, very free.

'Sunray' (74) MILNER 1872(?) British

A coloured foliage cv with cream and green leaves overlaid with magenta. The young growth is especially bright. Flowers are single, calyx cerise with rosy-mauve corolla. A very popular bedding out cv in former days and it probably would be still if it were more freely available. 'Sunray' was found as a sport on 'Tardif' by Rudd in 1862 and introduced to cultivation by Milner 'some years' later, hence the query about the exact date.

'Susan Ford' (185) CLYNE 1974 British
Calyx – bright rose, tube short, sepals reflex. Corolla – double, purple then light purple with the large individual petals attractively waved. This cultivar was raised by amateur grower Mrs Ivy Clyne from a cross between 'La Campanella' and 'Winston Churchill'. The flowers colour better in part shade in a hot climate. Upright, self-branching, bush or standard.

'Susan Travis' TRAVIS 1958 British
Two-tone pink single flowers. Hardy, upright to 1 m (3 ft). Said to bear the largest flowers for a hardy plant.

'Swanley Gem' (61) CANNELL 1901 British
Calyx – deep red, the sepals are held vertically. Corolla – single, violet then mauve. The petals spread out wide on the mature flower. Upright, bush.

'Swanley Yellow' (54) CANNELL 1900 British
Calyx – pinkish orange. Corolla

– single, orange-vermilion. Hardly yellow in the true sense of the word but a good colour all the same. Needs plenty of sun to get the best from the clusters of flowers. An interesting pot plant in any collection.

'Sweet Leilani' (164) TIRET 1957 American
Calyx – pale rose-pink with distinct recurving sepals. Corolla – single pale smoky-blue, very large petals. Upright, bush.

'Sweetheart' VAN WIERINGEN 1970 Netherlands
Tube – white; sepals – white with pink shading. Corolla – single, white shading at the base of the pink petals. Upright, floriferous. Will bed out well.

'Sweet Sixteen' (97) WALKER-JONES 1961 American
Double flowers a pleasing shade of rose-madder, wide spreading sepals. Trailer, can be trained to a variety of forms.

'Swingtime' (151) TIRET 1960 American
Calyx – bright red, short tube, spreading sepals. Corolla – double, glistening white with light pink veining. Free flowering and free branching. Upright, basket or standard.

'Swiss Miss' FUCHSIA FOREST – CASTRO 1963 American

Calyx – pink, sepals green tipped. Corolla – semi-double, white veined pink with slight pink flush to outer petals. The corolla in which the petals are slightly waved opens out almost flat. Trailer. Basket.

'Symphony' (193) NEIDERHOLZER 1944 American
Calyx – pale pink, sepals curve upwards in a graceful arc. Corolla – single, pale violet then soft lavender-pink. Strong grower with plenty of flowers of perfect shape. Will make a good standard or act as a contrast in a bedding-out scheme.

'Tahiti' SCHNABEL 1963 American
Calyx – pale pink, sepals sweep up. Corolla – double, rose-lake. Large blooms on a large plant. Upright, bush.

'Tahoe' (197) KENNETT 1964 American
Calyx – white, pink flush to sides of sepals. Corolla – semi-double, blue and deep orchid-pink then two-tone rose and mauve. Upright.

'Television' (174) WALKERJONES 1950 American
Calyx – white with pale pink on underside of sepals. Corolla – double, deep blue with splashes of pale blue and pink. A semi-trailer, it can form an upright bush with training and support.

'Temptation' (198) PETERSON 1959 American
Calyx – white. Corolla – single rose shaded with orange, white base to petals. The blooms of medium size are carried with abandon. Upright, bush.

'Tennessee Waltz' (186) WALKER 1950 American
Calyx – deep rose-red, sepals curve at tips. Corolla – double, rose-mauve with light red veins. Large flowers on a plant of good constitution, fairly hardy. Upright, bush.

'Texas Longhorn' (6) WALKER 1960 American
The semi-double white corolla of this striking plant is held in four very long, narrow sepals bright red in colour. Trailing but strong enough to be trained upwards.

'Thalia' (182) TURNER 1855 British
Long tubular single flowers produced in clusters, orange-scarlet. The plant is of *F. triphylla* appearance although it does not appear that this was one of the parents. Will bed out well when in a sunny place and the bronze green foliage will prove an added attraction.

'That's It' FUCHSIA-LA 1968 American
Calyx – pale orange-red. Corolla – double, medley of pink, purple, silver, pale red becoming 'smoky' rose when the bloom matures. Trailer, bush.

'The Doctor' (**129**) BROWN 1934 British
Calyx – pale rose, long tube. Corolla – single, deep salmon. Large, soft, light green foliage. Very vigorous; will make an imposing standard.

'The Phoenix' TIRET 1967 American
Calyx – deep rose-red, very long narrow sepals. Corolla – lilac-mauve, large blooms. Trailing, basket.

F. thymifolia see note under *F. x bacillaris.*

'Tiffany' (**79**) REEDSTROM 1960 American
Calyx – white striped mauve with pale pink flush to underside of broad, upturned sepals. Corolla – double, white with outer petals palest pink. On the mature bloom these petals roll inwards to form a series of tubes. Basket, bush.

'Tiki' BARTON 1970 New Zealand
Calyx – glowing coral red, sepals broad, long, reflexed. Corolla – double, clear pink.

Upright, very vigorous. The tiki is a lucky charm originally worn by the Maoris to promote fertility but today frequently seen as a New Zealand national emblem offered to tourists in the form of a small brooch.

'Ting-a-Ling' (**109**) SCHNABEL 1959 American
White self colour. A flower of most attractive form with the sepals held high and the petals extended in a cupshaped corolla. The single flowers are produced in quantity from this upright fairly tall plant. To preserve the whiteness of the blooms it is essential to grow in a spot out of the sun or pink flowers will result.

'Tinker Bell' HODGES 1955 American
Calyx – white or pink, tube long, sepals turn back, carmine tips. Corolla – single, white veined pale pink. Medium size flowers in delicate shades. Trailing. Basket.

'Tolling Bell' (**132**) TURNER 1964 British
Calyx – scarlet, tube short, sepals thick. Corolla – single, white, long petals form a perfect bell-shape. Vigorous, upright.

'Tom Thumb' (**45**) BAUDINAT 1850 French
Calyx – red. Corolla – single,

deep mauve then rose-mauve. Very small blooms produced in vast numbers. Easy inside or out. Hardy.

'Tom H. Oliver' PENNISI 1972 American

Calyx – deep rose, tube short, sepals pink beneath, standing out. Corolla – double, dark ruby-red with pale rose base to petals, edges of the petals are attractively serrated. Suitable for training to different shapes from a basket to a standard.

'Torch' (183) MUNKNER 1963 American

Tube – creamy-pink with magenta stripes; sepals – shining pink, deeper on underside, broad. Corolla – double, purple-red centre, salmon outer petals, large blooms. Upright, showy plant.

'Trail Blazer' (180) REITER 1951 American

Calyx – magenta. Corolla – double, deep magenta then rose-purple. Flower is striking in colour and form being very long. Growth is trailing making the plant effective in a hanging basket.

'Trailing Queen' (138) An old cv, probably British

Calyx – light red with very long pointed sepals. Corolla – single, four large petals that separate and seem to hang indepen-

dently. A real trailing plant that is a colourful addition to the greenhouse staging. Cascade.

'Tranquility' (102) SOO YUN 1970 American

Calyx – off-white, sepals have rose flush beneath, green tips. Corolla – double, initially deep lilac and pink then red with pink patterns. Sepals turn back to display the waved petals on this large bloom; each has several colours. Trailer, bush.

'Trase' DAWSON 1959 British

Calyx – carmine-red. Corolla – double, white with heavy pink flush, pink veins. Bushy, free flowering. Hardy to 0.5 m (1 ft 6 in.).

'Traudchen Bonstedt' (181) BONSTEDT 1905 German

Clusters of long-tube light cream to salmon flowers. Narrow, soft, light green foliage. *F. triphylla* hybrid.

'Treasure' (168) NEIDERHOLZER 1949 American

Calyx – cream at first then pale rose. Corolla – double, violet-blue with silver highlights. Very large, well-filled flowers. Upright.

'Trewince Twilight' JACKSON 1972 British

Calyx – white, wax-like, sepals curl back Corolla – single, mauve then pink. Easy growing, free branching, upright. This and another cv arose as sports on 'Marin Glow'. The other plant in cultivation named 'Lilian Lampard' (**101**) although of separate origin appears similar in all respects.

F. triphylla West Indies (Section Eufuchsia)

Small bushy plant with the typical long tubed flowers of the group. Carried in clusters the blooms are deep orange-red paling toward the base of the tube, petals very short, stamens not exserted. A fine range of hybrids has been produced using this plant as a parent. The first fuchsia to be described and the species upon which the genus was founded.

'Tristesse' (**116**) BLACKWELL 1965 British

Tube – pale rose; sepals – rose tipped green. Corolla – double, lilac-blue. This seedling of 'Lilac Lustre' has an easy, free-branching way of growing. Upright, bush.

'Tropic(al) Sunset' ANTONELLI 1965 American

Small reddish bronze foliage. Semi-double flowers with carmine sepals and dark purple corollas. No pinching out required on this valuable colour foliage plant, best in bright sun. Trailing, basket.

'Tropicana' TIRET 1964 American

Calyx – cream to rose. Corolla – double – orange-pink, very full, short. Trailer.

'Troubador' WALTZ 1963 American

Calyx – crimson, wide sepals. Corolla – double, deep lilac-blue with a crimson area at the base of each petal. Trailer.

'Trudy' GADSBY 1972 British

Calyx – pale pink, sepals deeper on reverse, upturned. Corolla – single, cyclamen purple with flush of pink at the base of each petal. Bloom is reminiscent of 'Chillerton Beauty' but 'Trudy' is much neater in growth and improved flower colour. Hardy to 0.5 m (1 ft 6 in.).

'Trumpeter' (**177**) REITER 1946 American

Clusters of thick long tubed flowers, pale geranium lake in colour. Blue-green foliage. *F. triphylla* hybrid.

'Tuonela' BLACKWELL 1969 British

Calyx – pale pink with more colour on the undersides of sepals. Corolla – double, soft lavender with pink veins. Large flowers and leaves. Growth is strong but even so some support is advised to carry the weight of the blooms. Vigorous enough to make a climber.

'Tutone'   MACHADO   1963
American
Calyx – pink, Corolla – double, ashen blue or pink in alternate layers. Trailer.

'Ultramar'   REITER   1956
American
Calyx – creamy-white, sepals long, broad. Corolla – double, grey-blue with smaller white petals between the large true petals. Flowers globular in shape, very full. Upright, vigorous.

'Uncle Charley'   TIRET   1949
American
Calyx – red with sepals sweeping up. Corolla – semi-double, lavender-blue. An easy grower that does well when grown in several forms: a bushy summer bedder, a greenhouse pot-plant, or a standard.

'U.F.O.'   HANDLEY   1972   British
Tube – white; sepals – white with pink glow at their base at the point where they join the tube; the long sepals are held upright. Corolla – single, lavender-blue, paling at base of petals. These spread out to form the body of the U.F.O. Although of novelty appeal it is at the same time a very good plant for decorative effect. Upright, free.

'Upward Look'   GADSBY   1968

British
Calyx – bright carmine, sepals with green tips. Corolla – single, reddish purple. Small flowers that grow upwards resembling 'Bon Accorde', one of its parents. Free flowering as a greenhouse pot-plant.

'Valencia'   SCHNABEL   1962
American
Calyx – rose. Corolla – semi-double, vivid pink. Dark green foliage. Upright, bush.

'Vanity Fair'   SCHNABEL   1962
American
Calyx – greenish-white. Corolla – double, pale pink, globular, petals serrated with the centre resembling a carnation. Upright, bush.

'Violet Rosette'   KUECHLER   1963 American
Calyx – bright carmine with broad recurved sepals. Corolla – double, violet with red stain at the base of each petal. Strong spreading bush.

'Voltaire' (19)   LEMOINE   1897
French
Calyx – bright red with recurved sepals. Corolla – single, rose-carmine. Sturdy, upright bush.

'Voodoo' TIRET 1953 American
Calyx – dark red, short tube, long spreading sepals. Corolla – double, deep purple-violet. Upright, bush.

'War Paint' KENNETT 1960 American
Calyx – white, short tube, flaring sepals. Corolla – double, dianthus-purple with coral marbling then reddish-purple. Upright, bush.

'Wennington Beck' THORN-LEY 1974 British
Calyx – pink flushed over green sepals, underside clear soft pink. Corolla – double, soft lilac-blue shaded to pink at the base of petals. The petals have serrated edges which adds to the charm of the flower. Basket.

'Whirlaway' (13) WALTZ 1961 American
Calyx – white, sepals tipped green, very long. Corolla – semi-double, white with the merest pink flush when mature. A graceful plant with large blooms on thin arching branches. Trailer.

'White Ann' (67) WILLS 1972 British
A red and white, double flowered sport which occurred on 'Heidi Ann' and every bit as good as the original. Bush.

'White Fairy' (159) WALTZ 1963 American
This double flower is basically white with the merest flush to the underside of the mature sepals. The bright pink anthers emphasise the glistening white-ness of the petals. Upright, rather spreading.

'White Pixie' (41) RAWLINS 1969 British
Small red and white single flowers borne in profusion amid pale green almost yellow foliage. Hardy to 1 m (3 ft). A sport from 'Pixie'. This plant has produced similar sports in different places and although each should have a separate clonal name they appear to be identical.

'White Spider' (121) HAAG 1951 American
Tube – white striped red, short; sepals – white flushed pink, very long and twisting, sometimes rolling right up. Corolla – single, white then pale pink. One of the most easily recognised of all the fuchsias. An adaptable plant that at first seems suitable only for a basket but with training can be shaped to a bush or even a standard.

'Wings of Song' BLACKWELL 1968 British
Calyx – bright rose-pink. Corolla – double, lavender-pink with deep pink veins. Vigorous, cascade.

'Winston Churchill' (76) GARSON 1942 American
Calyx – bright rose-red. Corolla – semi-double or double, deep

lavender-blue then magenta, waved petals. Small dark green foliage. A fine show plant.

'W. P. Wood' WOOD 1954 British

Hardy plant with bright red and royal blue single flowers. Upright to 0.7 m (2 ft).

'Ziegfield Girl' **(175)** FUCHSIA FOREST 1966 American

Apart from the green tips to the sepals the large round blooms of this excellent cv are the clearest shade of shell pink. Trailer.

APPENDIX

Species of the genus *Fuchsia* arranged in their sections.
Key T=type plant C=plants in cultivation in Britain (i.e. species usually offered for sale).
These are the species and subspecies of *Fuchsia* as revised by Dr. Munz and Dr Breedlove.

1. Quelusia
campos-porti
bracelinae
magellanica var. *magellanica* T
         var. *macrostema* C
         var. *molinae* C
coccinea
regia var. *regia*
    var. *affinis*
    var. *alpestris* C
    var. *radicans*

2. Eufuchsia
abrupta
andrei
asperifolia
aspiazui
asplundii
austromontana
ayavacensis
boliviana var. *boliviana*
      var. *puberulenta*
      var. *luxurians* C
canescens
confertifolia
cordifolia
corymbiflora
cuatrecasasii
decussata
denticulata (*serratifolia*) C
fischeri
fulgens C
furfuracea
gehrigeri
glaberrima
hartwegii
hirtella
hypoleuca
jahnii
killipii
lehmannii
leptopoda
llewelynii

loxensis
macrophylla
macrostigma var. *macrostigma*
         var. *longiflora*
magdalinae
mathewsii
munzii
osgoodii ·
ovalis
pallescens
petiolaris var. *petiolaris*
       var. *bolivarensis*
pilosa
platypetala
polyantha
pringsheimii
putumayensis
rivularis
sanctae-rosae C
scabriuscula
sessilifolia
simplicicaulis C
smithii
splendens C
storkii
sylvatica
tincta
townshendii
triphylla T C
venusta var. *venusta*
      var. *huilensis*
verrucosa
woytkowskii

3. Kierschlegeria
lycioides

4. Skinnera
colensoi
cyrtandroides
excorticata T C
perscandens
procumbens C

5. Hemsleyella
apetala T
cestroides
decidua
garleppiana
hirsuta
juntasensis
macrantha
membranacea
salicifolia
tuberosa var. *tuberosa*
　　　　var. *inflata*
tunariensis
unduavensis

6. Schufia
arborescens var. *arborescens* T C
　　　　var. *tenuis*
　　　　var. *parva*

7. Encliandra
microphylla var. *microphylla* C
　　　　var. *hidalgensis*
　　　　var. *quercetorum*
　　　　var. *aprica*
　　　　var. *hemsleyana*
thymifolia var. *thymifolia* C
　　　　var. *minimaeflora* C
encliandra var. *encliandra* T
　　　　var. *tetradactyla*
obconica
parviflora
ravenii
x *bacillaris*

PEST CONTROL CHART

		Azobenzine	BHC	Captan	DDT
Aphids	Insects visible		S		D
Ants	Insects visible		D		
Black Root Rot	Sudden wilting			W	
Capsid Bug	Insects visible		S		D
Cyclamen Mite	Plant stunted		F*		D
Fuchsia Rust	Visible on foliage				
Grey Mould	Foliage falls			S	
Mealy Bug	Visible under curled foliage		S		
Red Spider Mite	Foliage dries then falls	F			
Thrips	Foliage 'peppered'		S		
White Fly	Insects visible		D		D
Vine Weevil	Unhealthy growth		D		

Key: S=Spray   S+ =Spray outdoors only   D=Dust
W=With water after attack   F=Fumigate   F*=Fumigate after attack
F+ =Fumigate at low overnight temperature

DDT/BHC	Derris	Malathion	Maneb	Nicotine	Petroleum Oil	Tecnazine	Thiram	Zineb
F	S	S+		S	S			
F								
								S
F		S+		S				
		D						
			S				S	S
						D, F+	S	
F S		S+			S			
	S			F				
F S	S			S, F	S			
F				F				
F*		W						

PRINCIPAL FUCHSIA SOCIETIES

Australia
Australian Fuchsia Society:
A. Snewin Esq.,
Box No. 129,
Rundle Street P.O.,
Adelaide S.A.5000.

Canada
British Columbia Fuchsia Society:
Mrs E. I. Hood,
2175 West 16th Avenue,
Vancouver 9,
British Columbia.

Ethiopia
Horticultural Society of Ethiopia:
Mrs Innes Marshall,
P.O. Box No. 1261
Addis Ababa.

Germany
Deutsche Dahlien und Gladiolen Gesellschaft:
674 Landau i d Pfalz,
Den Altes Stadhaus,
Koln.

Great Britain
The British Fuchsia Society:
C. H. Leytham Esq.,
72 Ash Lane,
Hale,
Altrincham,
Cheshire.

Holland
Nederlandse Kring van Fuschia Vrienden:
Mrs H. Wit-Nijhuis,
Oranje Nassaulaan 32,
Bilthoven,
The Hague.

New Zealand
Canterbury Horticultural Society Fuchsia Circle:
W. McNickel Esq.,
100 Richardson Terrace,
Opawa,
Christchurch 2.

Rhodesia
Fuchsia Society of Rhodesia:
Mrs V. Tomlinson,
31 Rossal Road,
Greendale,
Salisbury.

South Africa
South African Fuchsia Society:
Mrs J. Smith,
P.O. Box 227,
Gillitts,
Natal.

United States of America
American Fuchsia Society:
Hall of Flowers,
Garden Center of San Francisco,
Golden Gate Park,
San Francisco,
California 94122.

SELECT BIBLIOGRAPHY

A Revision of the Genus Fuchsia (*Onagraceae*), Dr Philip A. Munz, California Academy of Sciences, 1943
Fuchsias, E. J. Goulding, Bartholomew, 1973
Fuchsias, George Wells, Royal Horticultural Society, 1972
Fuchsias, Stanley J. Wilson, Faber and Faber, 1965
Fuchsia Culture, James Travis, Travis
Lovely Fuchsias, A. G. Puttock, John Gifford, 1959
Wagtail's Book of Fuchsias, Eileen Saunders, Wagtail's Publications, *Vol I*, 1971, *Vol II*, 1972, *Vol III*, 1973

GLOSSARY

Gardening and botanical terms used in the book.

Anther   The swollen part at the end of the filament containing the pollen.
Axil   The angle between stem and leaf from which new shoots or flowers spring.
Berry   The fleshy fruit.
Break   To branch, send out new growth from dormant wood.
Calyx   Sepals and tube together, the outer part of the flower.
Compost (1)   Correctly formulated garden soil used for potting.
Compost (2)   Correctly rotted down garden refuse etc. A valuable source of humus.
Corolla   Collective term for the petals.
Cultivar   Often abbreviated to cv or cvs (plural) this is the internationally accepted title for a 'man-made' garden plant.
Filament   The stalk of a stamen.
Inflorescence   The complete flower.
Mutate   *see* Sport.
Node   Leaf-joints on a shoot, usually slightly swollen.

Ovary The part that contains the ovules which, after fertilisation, become the seeds. The ovary then swells to become a berry.

Pedicel The flower-stalk.

Petal One of the floral 'leaves' which together make up the corolla.

Petaloid A part of the flower which becomes petal-like in form, usually a stamen which develops a tiny petal-like appendage. Sometimes also used to describe the outer, reduced petals of the double corolla.

Pot-back Re-pot a plant into a smaller sized pot than the one used the previous season.

Petiole Leaf-stalk.

Pot-on Re-pot a plant into a larger sized pot.

Sepal(s) Together with the tube form the calyx.

Sport A bud mutation which very often gives rise to a new cultivar.

Stamen Filament and anther together, the male portion of the flower.

Stigma The top of the style which being sticky allows pollen grains falling on it to adhere.

Stop Take out the growing tip.

Style The stalk which carries the stigma, together with the ovary forming the female part of the flower.

Tube Correctly known as the hypanthium, it is the elongated part of the calyx. The tube and ovary are joined until the flower fades.

INDEX

of plants described

Bold figures refer to colour illustrations. Figures in roman type refer to page numbers.

'Abbé Farges' **48**, 147
'Achievement' 147
'Aileen' 147
'Alaska' **123**, 147
'Alfred Rambaud' 147
'Alice Hoffman' **117**, 147
'Alison Ryle' **189**, 147
'Alyce Larson' **39**, 147
'Ambassador' **125**, 147
'Americana Elegans' 147
'Amy Lye' 148
'Andenken an Heinrich Henkel'
   ('H. Henkel') 148
'Andrew' **124**, 148
'Angela Leslie' 148
'Angel's Flight' 148
'Aquarius' 148
arborescens var. *arborescens* **137**, 148
'Arabella' **190**, 148
'Army Nurse' **74**, 149
'Arthur Cope' **142**, 149
'Athela' 149
'Australia Fair' 149

x bacillaris 149
'Balkon' **36**, 149
'Balkonkonigen' **36**, 149
'Ballet Girl' 149
'Bella Forbes' 149
'Bellbottoms' 150
'Bernadette' **11**, 150
'Beauty of Bath' **95**, 150
'Billy Green' **184**, 150
'Bishop's Bells' 150
'Bland's New Striped' 150
'Blue Bush' 150
'Blue Butterfly' 150
'Blue Lagoon' 150
'Blue Mist' 150
'Blue Pearl' 151
'Blue Petticoat' 151
'Blue Pinwheel' 151
'Blue Sleigh Bells' 151
'Blue Waves' **25**, 151

'Blush of Dawn' **7**, 151
'Boerhave' 151
boliviana 151
boliviana var. *luxurians* **140**, 151
   'Alba' **141**, 152
'Bon Bon' **169**, 152
'Bonnie Lass' **37**, 152
'Bountiful' 152
'Bouquet' 152
'Bridesmaid' 152
'Brigadoon' 152
'Brilliant' 152
'Brutus' **167**, 152

'Caballero' 153
'Caesar' **107**, 153
'Caledonia' **139**, 153
'Candlelight' 153
'Carmen' 153
'Carmen' (Blackwell) **2**, 153
'Carnival' 153
'Caroline' **161**, 153
'Cascade' **59**, 154
'Celia Smedley' 154
'Centerpiece' **8**, 154
'Chang' **126**, 154
'Charlie Girl' **99**, 154
'Charming' **152**, 154
'Checkerboard' **16**, 154
'Chillerton Beauty' **42**, **43**, 154
'China Doll' 155
'China Lantern' 155
'Circe' 155
'Citation' 155
'Cliff's Hardy' 155
'Cloth of Gold' **72**, 155
'Cloverdale' 155
'Cloverdale Jewel' 155
'Coachman' **15**, 155
'Collingwood' **86**, 156
'Comet' **154**, 156
'Constance' 156
'Constellation' **170**, 156
'Coralle' **178**, 156

'Cordifolia' 156
'Corymbiflora' see *boliviana* var. *luxurians*
'Corymbiflora Alba' see *boliviana* var. *luxurians* 'Alba'
'Corsair' 156
'Cosmopolitan' **192**, 156
'Cotton Candy' **80**, 157
'Countess of Aberdeen' **92**, 157
'Crackerjack' **56**, 157
'Crimson Bedder' 157
'Crinoline' 157
'Curly Q' **32**, 157
'Curtain Call' 157

'Dainty Lady' **195**, 157
'Danny Boy' **85**, 158
'David Alston' 158
'David Lockyer' **18**, 158
'Derby Belle' 158
'Derby Imp' 158
'Diablo' 158
'Diana Wills' **94**, 158
'Display' 158
'Dilly Dilly' **130**, 158
'Dorothea Flower' **34**, 158
'Drame' 158
'Dunrobin Bedder' 159
'Dr. Topinard' 159
'Dusky Rose' 159
'Dutch Mill' **70**, 159

'Elizabeth' 159
'Empress of Prussia' **51**, 159
'Enfant Prodigue' 159
'Easter Bonnet' 159
'Evelyn Little' 159
excorticata 160
  'Purpurescens' 160

'Falling Stars' **31**, 160
'Fancy Pants' **160**, 160
'Fan Dancer' 160
'Fascination' 160
'Fiery Spider' 160
'Fiona' **58**, 160
'Flair' **145**, 161
'Flash' **46**, 161
'Flashlight' **62**, 161
'Flirtation Waltz' **12**, 161
'Florentina' 161
'Flying Cloud' **172**, 161

'Forget-me-Not' **33**, 161
'Forward Look' 161
'Frenchi' 161
fulgens 162
'Fulgens Speciosa' 184

'Gartenmeister Bonstedt' 162
'Gay Fandango' **131**, 162
'Georgana' 162
'Genii' 162
'Gloire de Marché' 162
'Golden Dawn' **120**, 162
'Golden Marinka' **75**, 162
'Graf Witte' **40**, 162
'Granada' **88**, 163
'Great Scott!' 163
'Grussaus dem Bodethal' **134**, 163
'Guinevere' 163

'Heart Throb' 163
'Heidi Ann' **66**, 163
'Heirloom' 163
'Henriette Ernst' **119**, 163
'Henri Poincaré' 163
'Hidcote Beauty' 163
'Hindu Belle' **179**, 163
'Howlett's Hardy' 164

'Ice Cream Soda' 164
'Iliusion' 164
'Impudence' **26**, 164
'Indian Maid' **98**, 164

'Jack Acland' 164
'Jack of Hearts' 164
'Jack Shahan' **57**, 164
'Jamboree' 164
'Joan Cooper' **28**, 164
'Joan Pacey' 165
'John Marsh' 165
'Joy Patmore' **64**, 165
'Juno' 165

'Kernan Robson' 165
'Keystone' **111**, 165
'King's Ransom' **68**, 165
'Kolding Perle' **127**, 165
'Kon Tiki' **82**, 166
'Kwintet' **65**, 166

'La Campanella' 166
'Lady Isobel Barnett' **63**, 166

'Lady Thumb'   166
'La Fiesta'   **22**, 166
'Lakeside'   166
'La Neige'   **187**, 166
'Laura'   **196**, 166
'Lena'   **77**, 167
'Lena Dalton'   **3**, 167
'Leonora'   **115**, 167
'Leverkusen'   ('Leverhulme')   167
'Leibriez'   **104**, 167
'Lilac Lustre'   **84**, 167
'Lolita'   168
'Lollypop'   **20**, 168
'Lonely Ballerina'   168
'Lord Lonsdale'   **122**, 168
'Lord Roberts'   **133**, 168
'Louise Emershaw'   **110**, 168
'Lovable'   **69**, 168
'Lucky Strike'   **147**, 168
'Lye's Unique'   **55**, 168
'Lyric'   **148**, 169

'Madame Cornelissen'   169
'Madame Van der Strass'   **14**, 169
magellanica   169
    alba   170
    'Conica'   169
    'Corallina'   169
    'Discolor'   169
    'Globosa'   169
    'Gracilis'   **47**, 170
    var. *macrostema*   **47**, 170
    var. *molinae*   170
    'Pumila'   170
    'Riccartonii'   170
    'Tricolor'   **44**, 170
    'Variegata' ('Gracilis Variegata')
        170
    'Versicolor'   **44**, 170
'Major Heaphy'   **52**, 170
'Mandarin'   **5**, 170
'Mantilla'   170
'Margaret'   171
'Margaret Brown'   171
'Margery Blake'   **73**, 171
'Marin Glow'   **91**, 171
'Marinka'   **128**, 171
'Mary'   **176**, 171
'Mieke Meursing'   **136**, 171
'Melody'   **1,108**, 171
'Merry Mary'   172
microphylla see x *bacillaris*

'Midnight Sun'   **158**, 172
'Minnesota'   **113**, 172
'Miss California'   **100**, 172
'Mission Bells'   172
'Molesworth'   172
'Monsoon'   172
'Moonlight Sonata'   172
'Morning Light'   **78**, 173
'Moth Blue'   173
'Mr A. Huggett'   **35**, 173
'Mr W. Rundle'   173
'Mrs Churchill'   **143**, 173
'Mrs Lovell Swisher'   **17**, 173
'Mrs Popple'   173
'Mrs Rundle'   173
'Muriel'   **194**, 173

'Nancy Lou'   174
'New Fascination'   174
'Nicola Jane'   174
'Nina Wills'   174
'Novato'   174

'Omeomy'   174
'Orange Drops'   174
'Orange Flare'   **135**, 174
'Orangy'   175
'Otherfellow'   **153**, 175

'Papa Bluess'   175
'Pathétique'   **81**, 175
'Pat Meara'   **9**, 175
'Peachy Keen'   175
'Peggy King'   175
'Pee Wee Rose'   **29**, 175
'Pepi'   **112**, 176
'Peppermint Stick'   **150**, 176
'Personality'   **149**, 176
'Phénoménal'   **27**, 176
'Phyllis'   **49**, 176
'Pink Balloon'   176
'Pink Bon Accorde'   **106**, 176
'Pink Chiffon'   176
'Pink Cloud'   176
'Pink Darling'   **38**, 177
'Pink Fairy'   **144**, 177
'Pink Flamingo'   177
'Pink Galore'   **60**, 177
'Pink Marshmallow'   177
'Pink Pearl'   **50**, 177
'Pink Quartette'   177
'Pink Temptation'   177

'Pinwheel' 178
'Pixie' 178
'Port Arthur' **188**, 178
'Prelude' **162**, 178
'Prince of Orange' 178
'Princess Dollar' **105**, 178
procumbens 178
'Purple Heart' 179

'Quasar' 179
'Queen Mary' **118**, 179

'R.A.F.' **146**, 179
'Rambling Rose' 179
'Raspberry' **103**, 179
'Red Ribbons' **71**, 179
'Red Shadows' 179
'Red Spider' **30**, 179
'Red Wing' 180
'Regal Robe' **83**, 180
regia var. *alpestris* 180
'Rhapsody' **171**, 180
'Rigoletto' **10**, 180
'Rosecroft Beauty' 180
'Rose of Castile (Improved)' **21**, 180
'Rose of Castile' **114**, 180
'Royal Purple' **53**, 181
'Royal Touch' **4**, 181
'Royal Velvet' 181
'Ruffled Petticoats' 181
'Ruffles' **173**, 181
'Rufus' **93**, 181

'Sally Ann' 181
sanctae-rosae 181
'San Diego' **87**, 181
'Sarong' **156**, 181
'Satellite' 182
'Sea Shell' 182
'Sensation' 182
'Shady Blue' **165**, 182
'Shady Lane' 182
'Shangri-La' 182
'Shasta' 182
'Shooting Star' **157**, 182
'Shy Look' 182
'Sierra Blue' **24**, 183
simplicicaulis 183
'Sleigh Bells' **89**, 183
'So Big' 183
'Snowcap' **166**, 183
'Sonata' **90**, 183

'Sophisticated Lady' **155**, 183
'Southgate' 183
'Speciosa' 184
'Spotlight' **199**, 184
splendens 184
'Spring Bells' **191**, 184
'Strawberry Delight' **23**, 184
'Strawberry Sundae' **96**, 184
'Summer Snow' 184
'Sunray' **74**, 184
'Susan Ford' **185**, 185
'Susan Travis' 185
'Swanley Gem' **61**, 185
'Swanley Yellow' **54**, 185
'Sweet Leilani' **164**, 185
'Sweetheart' 185
'Sweet Sixteen' **97**, 185
'Swingtime' **151**, 185
'Swiss Miss' 185
'Symphony' **193**, 186

'Tahiti' 186
'Tahoe' **197**, 186
'Television' **174**, 186
'Temptation' **198**, 186
'Tennessee Waltz' **186**, 186
'Texas Longhorn' **6**, 186
'Thalia' **182**, 186
'That's It' 187
'The Doctor' **129**, 187
'The Phoenix' 187
thymifolia see x *bacillaris*
'Tiffany' **79**, 187
'Tiki' 187
'Ting-a-Ling' **109**, 187
'Tinker Bell' 187
'Tolling Bell' **132**, 187
'Tom Thumb' **45**, 187
'Tom H. Oliver' 188
'Torch' **183**, 188
'Trail Blazer' **180**, 188
'Trailing Queen' **138**, 188
'Tranquility' **102**, 188
'Trase' 188
'Traudchen Bonstedt' **181**, 188
'Treasure' **168**, 188
'Trewince Twilight' 188
triphylla 189
'Tristesse' **116**, 189
'Tropic Sunset' 189
'Tropicana' 189
'Troubador' 189

'Trudy'   189
'Trumpeter'   **177**, 189
'Tuonela'   189
'Tutone'   190

'Ultramar'   190
'Uncle Charley'   190
'U.F.O.'   190
'Upward Look'   190

'Valencia'   190
'Vanity Fair'   190
'Violet Rosette'   190
'Voltaire'   **19**, 190
'Voodoo'   190

'War Paint'   191
'Wennington Beck'   191
'Whirlaway'   **13**, 191
'White Ann'   **67**, 191
'White Fairy'   **159**, 191
'White Pixie'   **41**, 191
'White Spider'   **121**, 191
'Wings of Song'   191
'Winston Churchill'   **76**, 191
'W. P. Wood'   192

'Ziegfield Girl'   **175**, 192